Daddy

A 21st Century Father's Approach to Pregnancy and Childbirth

Becoming a Connected Partner in the Journey

By: W. Bryan Caldwell, PE

www.daddydoulaish.com

Table of Contents

Forward:
A Letter from The Mother Who Endured It All

The birthing experience has changed so much from when I was born. Even the most wonderful of fathers typically played a minimal role in the delivery of his children. My mom tells each of her children their birth story annually on our birthdays. A highlight of my story is the moment she tells my wonderful dad that her water has broken and that she is in labor. His repose was, "do I have time to make coffee?" It is a family joke now, but priorities have clearly changed. The days of men sitting in the waiting room at hospitals while their beloveds brave the birthing journey alone are long gone. As our societal norms evolve it has been such a joy to watch my own husband embrace the role of fatherhood wholeheartedly and with such zeal.

When we discovered we were expecting our first baby I remember vividly how the color left his face and it took several hours to return. We were both in a bit of shock at the adventure that awaited us. As we prepared to become parents a shift began to take place in us both. Initially, I was completely content to have a fully, and I do mean FULLY, medicated delivery. As I began to research more, read more and open my mind to other possibilities, a change began to occur. The desire to do what was best for someone other than myself was beginning to take seed in my heart in a much deeper and fuller way than I had ever experienced. While I was going through this transformation my husband was also preparing his heart for our new addition. I can vividly remember one afternoon that I suggested we watch a documentary titled "The Business of Being Born" upon the recommendation of a friend. After 2 hours of this very detailed expose on various forms of birth the film ended with a feature on water births. I think my eyes were about to fall out of my head at this point with the looming knowledge of what my body was about to endure. When the program ended, I looked over at my husband and I swear I saw the glimmer of a tear in his eye as he said emphatically "it was so beautiful!" I was utterly shocked! I was also terrified that he would want to birth our baby in the living room, but the most overwhelming feeling was comfort and joy knowing that my husband was going to be a fully engaged partner in the birthing experience, and ultimately the parenthood experience.

Having gone through all three of our children's deliveries unmedicated and with my devoted husband by my side has strengthened our bond to one another and to our family in immeasurable ways. There are moments in your life when memories are eternally seared into your brain. The laugh of a beloved grandparent, a taste or smell that arouses all the memories of a place or time, the affirmation of an adored parent, the moment you walk towards your partner down the aisle, the joy of meeting your children. Memories that you will always hold in your heart and that can never be taken from you. For me, looking over at my husband in the 28th hour of intense labor, seeing his encouraging eyes and holding his hand has been eternally seared into my brain. What a gift to have a partner by your side to the bitter end, in labor, parenthood and in life. Being a fully engaged birth partner is an opportunity to establish or reaffirm your commitment to one another, your precious baby and to the family that you are building right from the get-go.

The saying that is so often used that "you get what you give" is applicable in all areas of life and not excluding labor/delivery and parenthood. Although the process of delivery is to be sure arduous, the elation and the overflow of joy and relief is worth every minute. Perhaps the greatest gift a parent can give their kids is to be fully engaged and checked in. Not just clocked in, but checked in. Be more than present, be engaged. This is what my husband and I are so passionate about in life and in parenthood. His passion has led him to pen this book to share the transformative experience of becoming a father and attempt to engage other men in their own fatherhood role. I am so proud of the work and dedication he has put into writing Daddy Doula. It is only a small glimpse into the devotion he has to his wife and his family. We are so grateful to call him ours.

Chapter 1:
A New Item On My Life's To-Do List

I don't even know how to describe how I feel as a father and husband now that I have helped bring three amazing bundles of wrinkly love into the world. The first thought that comes instantly to heart is that I am completely astonished that my wife delivered each of the girls with minimal intervention by the doctors. Each child was brought into this world as naturally as you can in this modern day of technology and medicine. The more I reflect on all that she endured during the pregnancy and that she delivered each one vaginally without any pain relief, I realized that I actually fell in love with her all over again. It is not the kind of love that I had when I realized she was "The One" and I was smitten with every flick of her dark hair, but the kind of love that reshaped my heart for her. My new love was a mixture of being awestruck by her resiliency in the pain of labor, a little sense of pride in that I can say "My wife did it the ol' fashion way", and a whole lot of being deeply connected to her in an emotional journey for three of the biggest moments in our lives.

I also have this inkling that I am a little bit more fulfilled as a man. Not the kind of man that can bench-press a Volkswagen or overcome his fears of falling out of an airplane, but more like the kind of man that sacrifices for the better moment for the ones he loves. It's like a box on my Life's To-Do List unexpectedly appeared in my heart and it was suddenly marked complete. I would call it "Redefine your Love" Box. I would not have known that such box existed in my heart, or even that it needed to be there. But sure enough, after 22 hours of grueling labor, my wife brought my first child into the world and for a brief moment my partner looked at me with thankful and adoring eyes. Right then I understood that I had changed and that our relationship had changed. The Redefine Your Love Box was suddenly a part of my character and changed what I wanted out of life. It took other high priority items like surfing in Hawaii, killing a deer with a bow and arrow, or going to the Barclay's Premier Soccer Championship and made them ancillary to helping my wife have a medication free vaginal delivery for the next baby. Even though I have not checked off any other items on the list, nor know the emotions or memories each item might bring, my experience during each pregnancy and childbirth has branded my soul. The deliveries of my children will most likely be one of the greatest total experiences of my life.

You might have the question, why did my wife's vaginal birth, without pain medication, make such a profound impact on me; especially since I was not the one actually experiencing the labor and delivery? I believe that to survive and overcome a moment of extreme adversity, a person and/or a team requires a different level of mental and physical prowess to come out the other end successfully. My wife and I took on the pregnancy and labor as a team. At the end of 9 months of pregnancy and 22 hours of labor, our experience redefined us for the better. I learned how to empathize for her when she was going through physical, emotional, and hormonal adversity. She learned that I would support her and care for her through any crisis. I believe if she had her body numbed to the natural process, she would have cruised through delivery without experiencing the intense sensations and emotions of childbirth. In turn, I would not have experienced her strength and beauty in that moment. Our preparation for the birth would have seemed to be a waste of time and the moments in the delivery room would have just slipped by without any tangible feelings or memories of the greatest stories of our lives.

So how and when did the "Redefine your Love" appear on my Life To-Do List. It was not an instant manifestation. It happened slowly over the term of the first pregnancy. After my wife and I found out she was pregnant and that the pregnancy was viable, we began to plan for the inevitable due date. At this point I assumed I would be expected to help around the house and be responsible for getting ice cream and pickles at late hours of the night. I also assumed when the actual contractions started and the infamous water broke, I would just turn her over to the doctors and the other women in her life for delivery. The medical team would work their mystical powers and get my wife through the delivery. My pop culture understanding of the world said that a baby delivery was generally a standard practice in the modern world of medicine. All the mother had to do was make it to the hospital. Then the baby would drop into the hands of the doctor after working her medical magic. It stands to cultural reasoning all the man had to do was wait patiently in the adjacent room, or beside the delivery room door, to claim his legacy.

Here is a quick glance at the way I understood the pregnancy and childbirth prior to my first daughter being born:

- Partner eats weird food combinations as her body transforms.
- At some point after 9 months, the water breaks.
- Contractions begin.
- The woman goes to the hospital in a mad scramble and gut-wrenching screams.
- Once she is checked in, she will be given an epidural that basically makes her body completely numb to the pains of the contractions and the cursing stops.
- The doctors and nurses work their medical magic and a few hours later the baby is born.
- Once the baby is born, I would be taken to the room to see a happy mother and a new crying baby.

Gentleman, that short tale of a pregnancy and childbirth is mostly fiction. I first discovered this uninformed birth process was not in the realm of reality when my wife and I watched our first birthing documentary. Because I am an Engineer by trade, I like to know the variables in my designs and know how each can affect the results of my creation. When it came to giving birth, I did not even know what the variables to childbirth were or how they dictated the experience. After a few moments on "The Google" I found some documentaries that were provided by some content providers. Like most people these days, my wife and I snuggled in on the couch for the night and binge watched all of them.

Each of the films below provides some history and different perspectives on childbirth:

- National Geographic: In The Womb
  http://topdocumentaryfilms.com/natio...c-in-the-womb/

- National Geographic: The Science of Babies
  http://channel.nationalgeographic.co...nce-of-babies/)

- Natural Born Babies - Modern Day, Natural Childbirth
  (http://amzn.to/18XIvEe)

- Discovery Health: The Ultimate Guide: Pregnancy
  http://youtu.be/J5TJfZUAETA

- Business of Being Born (Netflix)

- More Business of Being Born (Netflix)

The film that impacted my wife and I the most was titled "The Business of Being Born". We were probably drawn to it first because the film was based on a pop celebrity. Ultimately after watching the documentary, I was slapped into reality with such a dumfounding thunder that I instantly understood how deep my birthing ignorance ran. The documentary showed women giving birth in their homes with the help of midwifes and doulas coaching them through the Labor and Delivery (L&D). I was really shocked when I saw a water birth in a "kiddy pool". The documentary gave the full audio compilation of women experiencing labor contractions, the associated pain induced moans, and ultimately their baby being born. The film was so personal and real that it became a little terrifying for my wife to see the women go through so much pain. But I also believe during the film a sense of admiration developed for the women because they were able to endure. For me it was an amazingly crazy spectacle. I was so impressed by the strengths and will-power of the women. It was something extraordinary to witness for the first time. It was truly a front row seat to the gateway of life. The documentaries deeply inspired us to follow in the footsteps of other courageous women.

I want to clear up a few terms that I just used that may have elicited a picture of a feisty old woman in a long black dress calling for hot towels, a chamber pot, and for all the men to scram as she begins working with the screaming woman who is in the middle of giving birth: Midwife and Doula. Once you watch any of the above listed documentaries you will have a better understanding of a modern Mid Wife and Doula and their function in labor and delivery. But to help you now, I will give you the laymen's definition of each.

Midwife: A specialist who is usually a Registered Nurse concentrating their discipline in pregnancy, childbirth, postpartum and women's sexual and reproductive health. They can recognize the variations in the normal progression of labor and how to deal with deviations from normal delivery. The Midwife can discern what non-invasive actions are required for high risk situations. Examples would be when the baby presents breech (butt first) or when the baby is in a posterior position (head up or sunny side up). The big take a way is that they are **medically educated and trained**.

Doula: A birth companion and post-birth supporter that is a **nonmedical** person who specializes and assist a mother in the before, during, and/or after childbirth by providing physical assistance and emotional support. They typically have gone through certification classes that give them Professional Accreditation but are not trained to handle medical emergencies above that of basic First Aid. Most of the prominent doulas will have certifications by DONA International and CAPPA (Childbirth and Postpartum Professional Association) Doula certifications.

Earlier I mentioned there were variables in the labor and delivery process that I did not know were a part of the discussion. From the documentaries, I gleamed the most significant variables associated with the physical delivery were the following:

- Location of Birth: Hospital → Birthing Center → Home

- Birthing Position: Standing Birth → Sitting on All 4s → Lying on Back → Water Birth

- Medication: Anesthesia →Natural childbirth

Some of the positions associated with delivery might seem a little out there, but as you become more familiar with labor and delivery, your partner might even become comfortable enough to try a home birth in a pool.

There were a few other variables that some of the documentaries brought to my attention that I had never fathomed could play a role in the overall health of the baby. The films provided insights into the benefits of an unmedicated vaginal delivery such as the baby's increased ability to feed and sleep because oxytocin was excreted by the mother during labor. Oxytocin, also known as the bonding hormone, is absorbed by the baby while connected to the umbilical cord and is activated in the baby immediately after the birth with skin to skin contact and breast feeding. At first, I was a little skeptical, but after researching a few sites like *www.allparetning.com* and having a conversation with our OBGYN (doctor), there was really no reason to doubt the benefits of an unmedicated vaginal birth to both the mother and baby.

Additional benefits of a non-medicated vaginal birth are:

1. There are no risks of side effects caused by a medication such as irregular heart rates and critical breathing patterns by the baby and/or mother. Or some freak accident like becoming paralyzed after receiving an epidural anesthetic.

2. Mothers and babies are less groggy and can typically begin breast feeding immediately.

3. Mothers tend to feel a deep satisfaction, sense of empowerment, and even feelings of great pleasure with their labor experience. The experience can lessen the severity of postpartum depression and anxiety.

A few websites that I found helpful to understand more about vaginal births are:

- www.babycenter.com/natural-childbirth

- www.naturalbirthandbabycare.com/natural-birth

- http://www.ncbi.nlm.nih.gov/pmc/articles/PMC1595040/

After the documentary binge session, I found that the films had been impactful and that I had a new understanding of the birthing experience. I also had a clearer picture of the raw power and emotion of childbirth, as well as new perspective on how women have been bringing the human race into the world for millions of years.

Along with the enlightenment of real natural childbirth came a sense of wonder and the desire for my wife to deliver vaginally without pain medication. The imagery and influence of the films were so dramatic, that my wife decided that she wanted the unique experience of having a vaginal unmedicated childbirth. But at a hospital of course! Having a home birth without a tried and tested OBGYN nurse in your corner seemed to make an unmedicated birth more daunting of a challenge for her first experience.

Over the next few days my wife started doing lots of research about unmedicated vaginal births. Among the many experiences she wanted as part of her labor and delivery, she decided she was going to deliver in the hospital, and she wanted to hire a doula for guidance and support. Since we were going to the hospital a Midwife was not necessary because the doctor would be available. With the security of the hospital staff and technology around to ease her fears of complications in the baby and herself, she felt that a doula was key to the birthing process. The doula's support would help her to mentally make it through the stages of delivery. My wife had a few friends and her older sister had tried using a doula. They all gave her positive feedback and encouraged the benefits of a doula's support.

Like most husbands, I wanted to please my wife, but I was skeptical about having a doula because I did not understand how the doula would actually be a benefit to her during the delivery. Because I am frugal (okay cheap is better way to describe my monetary policy), I was very apprehensive about paying $500 to $2000 for the service. Based on some quotes from local doulas, generally a Doula Service includes 2 to 3 consultations between my wife and the doula that allow them to emotionally connect with birth exercises. Then the doula would be on call to either meet us at the house or the hospital when the contractions started. No matter how many times my wife described how the visits were setup, in my mind, the consultations were more like two distant friends meeting for a palates class to catch up. The more I thought about the doula being at the hospital, I gradually became irritated that some stranger was going to coach my wife though the labor and delivery while I sat in the corner. What was I supposed to be doing? I didn't want to be left out and rendered useless.

After a few conversations about the doulas she had found and me noticing how excited she was about this birthing experience, one night one of our conversations changed the direction of our childbirth journey. It went something like this:

Wife: I have found a few doulas that I want to interview. I am so excited we are doing this!

Husband: What exactly are we doing? And what exactly is a doula?

Wife: We are hiring a professional to help through the contractions so I can have an unmedicated birth. She is trained to assist me before, during, or after childbirth. The doula can provide me physical assistance, delivery techniques, and emotional support.

Husband: What exactly will you and the doula do?

Wife: She and I will make appointments over the term of the pregnancy where we get to know each other, create a birth plan, and practice labor techniques. During labor and delivery, she will coach me through the contractions and the pushing.

Husband: Why exactly do you need a doula?

Wife: Because I need someone I can trust, who will be emotionally supportive and who has been trained to get women through the birthing process.

Her trust statement hit me like a Mike Tyson body shot.

Husband: But wait, I am your husband. I can do all those things and we don't have to spend any money. How hard can it be? I saw the documentary. I want to do it! Most doulas are not trained healthcare professionals anyway, and we are going to the hospital. I can be all those things you need me to be. I will do whatever it takes to help you deliver our baby girl!

Wife: I don't know. It would be great for you to be a part of labor and delivery. (Head Cocked and one eyebrow raised) Okay. But you have to promise me you will be sweet and really try to learn a lot.

And at the end of that conversation this apparently manifested in my heart on my Life's Things To-Do List:

- Redefine your Love
- Understand all variables about the pregnancy and labor and the delivery
- Get connected to the pregnancy
- Become really sweet and learn how to communicate that sweetness in a tense situation

I think ego played a part in all the boxes appearing. My feelings were hurt when my wife did not believe I could be emotionally supportive or sensitive enough to get her through the labor. Beyond my pride, I also found myself in the moment when I had

21

the option of either being a bystander or being a full participant in something that was bringing my child into the world. I could choose to be present in this amazing journey or just keep moving along never looking up.

Because you are reading this book, I imagine you are experiencing a combination of excitement, dread, and anxiousness about the recent news that you are going to be a father (unless you are just one proactive dude). I know I did not have that movie like reaction that was all sweet gushy and rock steady when I found out I was going to be a father. It was more like a halfcocked smile mixed with a nervous sweat where I stood silent as 1000 thoughts of joy, disaster, and an empty bank account, ran through my mind before I fell into my wife's arms. I bet you have a hundred questions about the pregnancy and even more about how your partner is going to deliver the baby. The good news for you is that in an internet information world, there is more access to information than any philosopher or scientist in history. The bad news is there is just as much bad information out there to confuse anyone or scare you crazy. I would presume what is giving you the most heartburn is that you and your partner are considering an unmedicated vaginal birth and you doubt that you are capable of taking on the role of an active participant in the pregnancy and childbirth. The idea of this supportive man who can be the rock and emotional guide for his partner during labor has captured your imagination and inspired your emotions. It is possible that you fear that you might fall short of her expectations during the pregnancy and during childbirth. Sir;

I emphatically promise that if you take part in this moment of your life, there is no failing. You do not have to have the qualifications and birth experience as a certified doula to meet her expectations. You just have to try and have to learn. This book will not make you a certified doula, but it will make you Daddy Doula-ish. If you learn the basics of this book, take to heart the idea of becoming connected to your partner, and directly participate in the childbirth, the moment your partner is holding your child, the "-ish" falls off your ranking and can you can be called a Daddy Doula.

When framing your mind around the journey of becoming a Daddy Doula, remember it is an experience not a victory. It is a moment that cannot be appreciated by a Thumbs Up or a 52-character summary. It is a chance to experience what it is like to be human. To connect to something that does not give instant gratification and requires the heart of a Ronin Warrior. Even though the journey will be brief relative to the span of your life, it can become an epic tale that can shape who you are forever.

Chapter 2:
The Cement in the Foundation

To become the best Daddy Doula to your partner you must be mentally and emotionally present during the pregnancy. Being present creates the pathways between you and your partner to connect emotionally. Yes, we are going deep into the Jedi-hippy mind manipulation right out the gate. Stick with me, this chapter is the cement in the building of the book's foundation. We will get to the pregnancy stuff shortly. Think about it this way. You picking up this book is like taking on a construction project. Like all good building projects, once the foundation is built, everything else is constructed on and around it.

"Being present" has become a catchall phrase that sums up the concept in this chapter. The concept is more formally referred to as Mindfulness. The notion of Mindfulness is simple in idea but truly a mental mountain to overcome in our digital and social media world. Mindfulness is paying attention to the here and now with all your senses. When I started to learn how to observe the many moments of the day, I discovered that life is beautiful, weird, symmetric, chaotic, detailed, ironic, funny, and very colorful. I also began to observe that I have lots of anger inside of me that likes to rear its head when I feel guilty about my actions (past or present) or my intelligence is insulted. These personal revelations are the result of practicing Mindfulness regularly. As my Jedi-hippie mind becomes more powerful, I learn to take mental control over what I am feeling at any given moment and can be more focused on what is happening in the moment. Being able to identify negative emotions as it comes over me, but before they take control, have saved me from many arguments with my wife, coworkers, and others who like to push emotional buttons.

Before we get further into the matters of the mind, let me layout more clearly my definition of Mindfulness:

1. Being Mindful is being able to mentally stop to observe what is going on around you and in you with all your senses.

2. Once you stop, you can recognize that you are experiencing something in the now.

3. You can identify the physical sensation your body is experiencing.

4. You can understand the emotional, or spiritual, sensations that you might be having.

5. Ultimately you allow yourself to fully experience the moment and appreciate that you are human and that you are allowed to be in this moment.

Please understand that Mindfulness is not about only observing the cool breeze with roses in the air while suddenly feeling the warmth of your partners hand bring on the feeling the love. It also about noticing tension, anger, frustration, and emotional pain. The interesting and profound part about mindfulness is that if your mind can quickly identify emotions like anger and frustration, it will lessen the effects of the emotion and allow you to react more rationally. When the effects of the emotion are in check, you are less likely to blurt out those words you can't take back. Conversely, when happiness and joy are recognized, those moments become more tangible and rememberable. For a moment pause your reading and think about how you are feeling about this notion of Mindfulness.

What is the first word that pops into your mind?

Hopefully not **Bull Shit**!

Being Intentional

You might be asking yourself what exactly does it mean to be intentional in the context of "being present". So, Luke Sky Walker is standing on his hands with Yoda nested on his leg. When the camera pans out Luke is raising a rock using the force. He is intentionally being mindful of the energy flowing between him, the rock, and the ground and is able to levitate the rock. Once his concentration breaks, the pathways between each object collapses and each has to abide by the law of gravity. Bang! We all fall down. For the context of this book, to be intentional is to try some or all the recommendations of this book outlined in the following chapters. You will probably like a few and might think some are over-the-top. The goal is to try. Being intentional about the pregnancy tasks, knowing that you are blowing off guy time and lazy days on the couch for the duration of the pregnancy, is going to be hard. To be very honest here, 75% of the time I was the rock laying stubbornly in the swamp mud. On those days it was very frustrating for my wife, and most of the time I ended up alone feeling guilty. But the other 25% of the time, when I chose to engage with joyful intent, the resulting day always went better than expected and there seemed to be more affectionate reciprocation later in the evening. 1+1=2. I can only give you one guarantee in this book: if you engage the pregnancy with a joyful and open heart (an intentional act), then you will create a connection to the pregnancy.

Meditation Practice

You are probably thinking that Meditation is another Jedi-hippy-mind-manipulating charade that is propagated by fake gurus trying to make a buck with their self-help books. I was with you until I came across the Headspace® App. A little background. I have wanted to be an engineer since my first LEGO® set. But for some reason I have always been a B/C student. In high school I barely escaped with 3.0. I earned a 720 math and a 340 verbal on the SAT. Not good enough to get into Georgia Tech out of high school. I had to go the long way through community college and many other challenges of post high school. To make a long story really short and boring, when I eventually got on the path to becoming an engineer, I found that I understood the engineering concepts of my classes. Homework and labs took effort, but I typically provided good work. It was the tests that always kicked my ass. For some reason my mind just knotted up and I struggled with the questions. In hindsight, it turned out that I have severe test anxiety, or performance anxiety. It wasn't until I went through the steps of the Headspace Anxiety Series that I started to understand this debilitating emotion. After a few years of non-regular practice, I generally began to be able to recognize my emotions as they started forming during stressful moments of life. Sometimes with the success of diverting the negative outcome! When I started my Master's in Engineering program, I was able to put the practice of meditation to the test. The MS curriculum schedule required that I take one class every 8 weeks, which equates to a midterm of super anxiety every 4 weeks. Before my first test, about 30 minutes before the start, I was setting in the library waiting for my proctored room to come available. My hands were clammy, my chest felt like Darth Vader was squeezing his thumb and forefinger together. I was a complete pre-test anxious wreck. This time because of my meditation practice, instead of just withering in my panic, I quickly realized my symptoms, exited the library, and went back to my car. My heart rate monitor on my watch was reading 145 bpm. I cranked up the car, the ac, and my Headspace App. I chose a 15-minute performance session. When I opened my eyes after the last long exhale, my head was clear, and my heart rate was back to a normal 58 bpm. I confidently walked into the test, and 90 minutes later I grumpily walked out. I knew I did not make an "A" again, but I passed my first master level engineering test! Hey! not bad for the first test in 12 years. For the next 2 years, meditating prior to every test became habit. No matter how I felt about my preparation prior to the test, when I walked into the proctor room, I was calm and clear headed. It must have worked for the most part because I completed my Masters in Engineering Management with a 3.8. (Pat on Back)

So, what does meditation have to do with being a Daddy Doula? Meditation teaches you how to be present in yourself and the moment. It gives you tools to recognize the cues of your body when you start to get frustrated, annoyed, pissed-off, anxious, or other negative emotions prior to them consuming your actions.

Conversely, it can teach you to become enveloped in moments that are full of joy and love.

I have found that when I am in a good meditation practice, the craziest thoughts will cross my mind. The memories of a childhood bully (anger) or teenage love (regret) might resurface, or maybe anxiety about my job (performance). With your own practice, Meditation will teach you to recognize those thoughts for what they are and allow you to move past them for the moment. If you want to resolve those deep emotions later with a professional, you will be able to more easily because now you know how those experiences make you feel today. While practicing meditation you are teaching yourself not to dwell on any given thought or emotion, but just to recognize it.

If you do not want to learn meditation for more control over your mind, then my suggestion is to at least learn the techniques. The Headspace® app has a Basic Course that can get you started. The reason I want you to learn about the techniques is because in Chapter 5.5 Yoga Balls, Contraction Mediation, and Visualization I will utilize the breathing techniques to help your partner become more relaxed. It will make it easier for you and your partner if you are the coach.

Meditation and Mindfulness practice are essential to being a great Daddy Doula. I remember distinctly how I felt in the moment when my wife told me she was pregnant with our first child. My mindfulness practice instinctively kicked in and forced my subconscious to align to the moment. Once I was aware of my feelings and thoughts, I was able to experience the life of an expecting father completely, all be it a mixed bag of terror and joy. Being a Mindful partner allowed me to be a fully emotional and participating father during the pregnancy and in the labor-room. The results of maintaining that connection during the delivery changed me at my core. The Eureka moment I felt when I held my daughter for the first time was so powerful it compelled me to share my story with other expecting fathers like you. I knew that if I shared my stories of my approach to the pregnancy and childbirth with other expecting fathers, other fathers would learn the tools need to be a partner in the delivery room. Fathers might gain the confidence to try and open their hearts up to the possibility of having a real connection in their life that might seem illusive to them now.

Core Principles

I am passionate about this book and all that it has to teach. It is important that you understand the Why before we get to the How and What of being a Daddy Doula.

I consider myself fairly like most men in the world. A little rough around the edges, emotionally distant most of the time, and I am semi-competitive (i.e. prideful). This book is the result of "I wish I would have done it a different way". Especially for the first pregnancy and childbirth. I want other fathers to be more educated about the entire process and not have be in the dark like I was in the beginning. I desire for other fathers to want to grab a hold of this moment in their lives so that they have something to cherish in their hearts forever. So, if above is not clear of my Why this book exists, hopefully the next 3 principles will clear it up:

1. Connect to the moment with a heart full of love. Connecting emotionally with your partner will be the secret to her confidence in you as a Daddy Doula.

2. Experiencing the journey of the pregnancy and childbirth will leave you more fulfilled.

3. The vaginal unmedicated delivery of your baby is more fulfilling to the mother and to you. Promote the delivery process if it is safe for the mother and child.

That is the Why. In the subsequent chapters of this book you will learn the How and What it is to be a Daddy Doula. You will be given medical information, tools and insights to maneuvering the pregnancy and childbirth. I will help you blind yourself to the relentless distractions of the world and help you experience a truly unique moment in your life. No matter the obstacles of the pregnancy or the means your child is born, if you commit to this book, you will succumb to the overwhelming eruption of love that fills your heart on D-Day and that unique moment will be carved into your soul forever.

Chapter 3:
Labor and Delivery Terms to Be Familiar With

Imagine you are a brave explorer who has discovered some new amazing world. In your first encounter in this world you discover an indigenous people you call the Vorad who speak a never heard language you describe as Voronian. Because you are an experienced and well-travelled explorer, you know that to survive any adventure into an unknown world, you are going to have to learn about the customs of the Vorad. You will also need to learn how to communicate with them. Fortunately, during your adventures you encountered an old Vorad trader named Hoag who used to travel across the oceans to sell his exotic spices and Voradian Spirit to your world. Because Hoag's was a trader with your world, he could communicate basic English. You contracted him to guide you through this unknown world and to communicate with the shamans of the tribes. The shamans held all the knowledge of their world. They could tell you the plants that are medicines or poisons and where the wonders of the land could be found. Hoag was the man you needed to translate Voronian into understandable terms.

Welcome to the world of Pregnancy and Labor. I am your Hoag and I will be your guide. It is important that you can communicate at the same level as your partner when it comes to the pregnancy and childbirth. She will be having detailed conversations with her OBGYN where she will be learning extensively about the pregnancy and childbirth. If you can have a thorough discussion with her about her monthly prenatal checkups you will be able to take on a more active role in the pregnancy. I have created a list of terms below that will be used by the OBGYN during checkups, the later stages of the pregnancy, the planning of the delivery, and during labor. I am going to keep the information at a 30,000-foot level so that you and your partner can fill in the details together. If there is any confusion or uncertainty about a process or situation, always consult your OBGYN for more detailed information and guidance. Remember, your doctor's input and guidance are only as good as your questions, so your ability to speak Voradian is crucial when making decisions about the pregnancy and childbirth.

Cervix: Refers to the lower part of the uterus that connects to the vagina. It is like a throat, a narrow passage in the bottom of the uterus. This passage must expand before the baby can lower down into the birth canal.

Effaced (Effacement): Refers to the process by which the cervix thins and gets ready for delivery. The cervix gradually softens, shortens and becomes thinner when the baby moves into the birthing position. You might hear phrases like "ripens," or "cervical thinning" which refer to effacement. Effacement is measured in percentages. When your partner goes to her doctor in the last month of the pregnancy, the doctor will report the effacement. She might report that she is effaced 50%, which means the baby is moving down. When she is 100% effaced or completely effaced, the cervix is paper-thin, and the baby will come soon after.

Dilation: Refers to cervical dilation and is the opening of the cervix which accesses the baby to the birth canal. Dilation increases as the effacement increases. The cervical opening is measured in centimeters. The stage of labor is identified by the dilation.

- Pre-Labor: 0-3 centimeters

- Active Labor: 4-7 centimeters

- Transition: 8-10 centimeters

- Complete: 10 centimeters. Delivery of the infant takes place shortly after this stage is reached (although the mother does not always push right away.)

Doctors are trained on plastic O-Rings that are 1cm to 10Cm in diameter. The Doctors use their fingers tips to penetrate the O Ring to determine the dilation. Because every doctor's hands are different, it is about feel. Generally, a person's fingertips are around 1 cm in diameter.

Station: Refers to how far the baby is down in the birth canal. It is measured by the relationship of the baby's head to the mother's tail bone (to be exact the ischial tuberosity) and measured in negative and positive numbers. (-5 is a floating baby, 0 station is said to be engaged in the pelvis, and +5 is crowning)

When the nurses and doctors are examining your partner during labor you will hear numbers reported like 3/60/-3 which mean 3 centimeters dilated, 60% effaced, and at station -3; essentially that means there is still a lot of work to do before the baby is born.

The Bag of Waters: Also known as the amniotic sac in which the fetus lives and develops. It is a thin and tough pair of membranes that hold a developing fetus in the amniotic fluid until shortly before birth

Placenta: It is an organ that connects the developing fetus to the uterus to allow nutrient uptake and regulate temperature. It will provide oxygen and nutrients to growing babies and removes waste products from the baby's blood.

Umbilical Cord: It is a conduit between the developing baby and the placenta. It supplies the baby with oxygenated, nutrient-rich blood from the placenta.

Vaginal Delivery: A vaginal delivery is the movement of the baby from the uterus into the birth canal and out of the vagina. A vaginal delivery can be done with or without medical intervention. If a vaginal birth requires medical intervention it is referred to as an Assisted Vaginal Delivery. An assisted vaginal delivery could be as simple as the doctor bursting the bag of waters or as complicated as using equipment like forceps or a vacuum extractor to guide the baby out of the birth canal.

Medicated Delivery: Refers to the use of medications to either induce labor or to prevent the mother from experiencing pain or severe anxiety. These medicines which can also affect the baby. The use of a prescription drug for a pre-diagnosed condition, like controlling Mom's blood pressure, might be medically necessary but not generally considered a medicated delivery.

Pitocin: Pitocin is the synthetic version of the naturally occurring hormone oxytocin. When a woman goes into labor naturally, oxytocin is the hormone that is released by the body that kick starts the contractions. Pitocin is generally used by the doctor when labor has stalled or needs to be sped up for medical reasons.

Epidural: Refers to anesthesia that is administered to the lower back into the spine. It is a regional anesthetic which means it blocks pain in a particular region of the body. Epidurals block the nerve impulses from the lower spinal segments which results in decreased sensation in the lower half of the body, including the uterus.

Epidural medications fall into a class of drugs called local anesthetics, such as bupivacaine, chloroprocaine, or lidocaine. They are often delivered in combination with opioids or narcotics such as fentanyl and sufentanil in order to decrease the required dose of the local anesthetic. This combination produces maximum pain relief. In addition to the epidural, epinephrine, morphine, or clonidine maybe used to prolong the epidural's pain relief, or to stabilize the mother's blood pressure.

Inducing Delivery: Inducing involves the doctor or medical staff manually stimulating the mother's body to begin contractions. Manually thinning or bursting the bag of waters is considered a natural assist to inspire the mother's body to begin contractions. Administering Pitocin is considered to be a medicated assist to force the uterus to begin contractions

C-Section Delivery: A caesarian section is a surgical incision in the mother's abdomen and uterus. It is not a minor surgery! It involves moving around the internal organs of the mother to access the uterus where the baby is located. A surgically trained doctor has to perform the procedure. The baby is delivered by the doctor by reaching through the incision in the uterus and removing the baby. Because of the severity of the procedure, the mother will have to be put under anesthesia or will have had an epidural applied prior to the procedure. A C-section can be scheduled in advance because of known complications that could occur during delivery or can be done in response to an unforeseen complication. An example of an unforeseen complication is if the amniotic fluid is below acceptable range during contractions and the baby's heart drops to a dangerous level and does not recover after the contraction. Please consult with your OBGYN for examples of conditions that might require a C-section that will ensure the safety of the baby and mother.

Birth Plan: Refers to how the mother wants to approach the labor and delivery (L&D), and post-delivery. The plan will state if the mother will have natural childbirth, use pain medications, or other medical assistance during the labor, as well as post-delivery handling of the baby and the regime of vaccinations. It also outlines alternative options or interventions in case things do not go according to the original plan. You and your partner should develop this plan together with your doctor so that everyone from the beginning is on the same page. On D-Day (Delivery Day) you will usually provide the one-page game plan to the L&D team that will be assisting your partner during the birth and after delivery

There are Three Phases of Labor: Pre, Active, and Transition.

Pre-Labor: Refers to the early stages of the labor where your partner is experiencing contractions that are coming at random intervals and durations. This stage can last hours or days. It is not usually very intense for the mother. This phase is almost like the body's natural way of signaling the mother to get somewhere safe before the real show begins.

Active Labor: Refers to labor when your partner is experiencing contractions that are occurring at shorter intervals with longer durations and at a higher intensity. This phase is the body's way of using internal forces to stretch the cervix and open the hips into a position to make way for the baby's head.

2-1-1: Refers to the critical interval during Active Labor in which the contractions are at 2 minutes apart with a 1-minute long contraction followed by a 1-minute break in the contraction. When your partner starts having contractions you should pull out your stopwatch and journal to log the time and length of contractions.

The journal will help you stay focused and ease some of your nerves because you are monitoring her progress and contraction patterns. Once contractions are hitting the 2:1:1 pattern you should be on your way to the hospital or already there because the transition labor phase where the baby starts to exit the birth canal could start at any moment.

Transition Labor: Refers to the labor phase where the baby is fully engaged and moving out the birth canal. Your partner is at 10/100/+5 and is experiencing the most intense contractions. Her body is transforming internally and externally to make room for the baby. It is game time.

Chapter 4:
Childbirth - All the Variables Defined

Being a first-time dad is nerve-racking enough when you think about how your life is going to change once the baby is born. But when you think about how you will influence your child over a lifetime, you could become instantly overwhelmed. As a parent, I want to provide enough love and wisdom that will help mold my children into good human beings. I never would have thought that the first decision I would have to make with my wife is how the child is born.

Without considering the Sci-Fi world of "Test Tube babies" who are incubated in a lab, there are two ways in which your partner can bring your child into the world: Vaginally or Cesarean Section (C-Section).

Chapter 4.1:
Vaginal Childbirth

Because of the documentaries on Natural Childbirth, my wife was inspired to try and have our baby vaginally without the use of any medication. She was fully aware that the delivery would be extremely painful, and that medication could alleviate the pain. She also understood the risks associated with a vaginal delivery and that the following scenarios could happen with a vaginal delivery:

- Excessive tearing of the uterus and internal hemorrhaging due to the violent nature of the contractions or the position of the baby that could lead to her or the baby's death.

- The baby compressing its umbilical cord or even having the umbilical cord wrapped around its neck. This complication can cause decreased blood flow to brain and thus the decreased oxygen is risking the baby's life

- Overstressing both Mom's and the baby's hearts so that one or both may fail during the delivery.

- The complete tearing of Mom's perineum

Despite my wife's fear of the pain, or the anxiety associated with the possible delivery problems listed above, she wanted to have this unique understanding of bringing life into the world only a woman can gain with an unmedicated childbirth. She wanted to join the elite ranks of her mother and generations of other women who delivered their children with courage and resilience. She wanted to discover those same traits in herself.

To be clear my wife and I were not under any delusion about the risks of childbirth. In the very beginning, we made the concession that if she or the baby became endangered, we would immediately relinquish our reins on the labor and let the doctors take over to work their medical expertise. If death of either my wife or the baby was a possibility during labor, we did not care if medication and/or C-Section was the solution to get us all home safely.

Chapter 4.1:
Un-Medicated Childbirth

For some women, labor comes on quick and unrelenting with barely enough time to get to the hospital, much less into a L&D room, before the baby is born. For these women, there is barely a distinction between pre-labor, active labor, and transition labor. Consider these women lucky and the quick birth to be like a unicorn in the land of the Vorad. For most women, according to www.pregancy.com, pre-labor is between 12 and 14 hours, active labor is between 1 and 2 hours and transition labor between 5 minutes and 1 hour. (htt) With the varying durations provided, it is easy to see how the market for a doula's skills are required if a woman wants to have an unmedicated childbirth. In the current mostly female doula market, if you stick to the core goals of this book you might be the unicorn in the doula world. When Mom goes unmedicated during childbirth, you and the medical staff must be very patient. For some mothers, especially first-time mothers, it may take days or weeks to start pre-labor after the predetermined "totally scientific" due date. I hope you get my sarcasm here, because the actual due date is not an exact science. To determine your partner's due date, the doctor brings her in for a visit around week 12 to take fetal measurements. Based on the measurements, a chart is referenced, and a guess is made on the day of conception. This date might line up with a very clear memory of coitus because it was either so spectacular or so rare you can easily pinpoint the conception date. Most likely you and your partner are actively engaging in mattress Olympics, so the conception date becomes a little less precise. Either way, the doctor uses the measurements of the fetus, a guessed conception date and to determine due date and 36 weeks is added to the conception date. My advice here is be flexible around the actual due date. If your plans hold fast to the due date, you might get surprised with a rush to the L&D room a few weeks earlier than planned and you will not have completed your D-Day preparation described in later chapters. If you need the information now, skip ahead to that chapter.

Once pre-labor does start, it might take 24 hours before the contractions are occurring on regular intervals with enough strength, to consider her to have progressed to active labor. Once she is in active labor it might be another 24 hours of strong contractions before she hits the critical 2-1-1 interval. Right now, you might have a "muddy" idea of what to expect once labor begins and may be experiencing a little anxiety. Stick with me. By the end of this book you will be familiar with all aspects of the labor process. Knowledge inspires confidence and confidence in your knowledge will ease your anxiety. Ultimately, once you are in the moment you will have the ability to be patient like Yoda and make the wait for the trip to the L&D room a little less stressful for both you and your partner.

Stop! I am not downplaying the importance of a Due Date, just its accuracy. The delivery of a child literally has the element of life and death in the equation. There is a time for patience and a time for action. Once the baby is 5 to 14 days (the margin of error for the due date) past the estimated due date, there are increased risks to the baby's mortality. The life source of the baby in the womb is the amniotic sack and placenta. Each is designed to last for a 36 to 38-week time period. Eventually one or both will exceed its expected duration and the baby will run out of life support. When the mother gets into this late stage of pregnancy, the doctor will be monitoring the situation almost daily. If the doctor determines that it is time to force the delivery and induce labor, there are a few actions that can inspire the body to start contracting naturally before a medical intervention is introduced:

1. The doctor can use a finger to manually dilate the cervix usually 1 to 2 cm. Sometimes the larger opening allows the baby to apply additional force to the cervix which may cause the body to release oxytocin and kick start contractions.

2. The doctor can strip the membrane with a cue-tip like tool to make it thinner. This can be done a few times and it may cause some bleeding. Similarly, the thinner the membrane the more downward force on the cervix.

3. The doctor can break the Bag of Waters. This will drop the baby down as far as possible onto the cervix.

Note: the movies might have set us up for dramatic affect versus reality when it comes to the breaking of the bag of waters.

Typically, the bag of waters does not break until later stages of active-labor. Very few women will experience the movie like scenario of the bag breaking in a restaurant and then proceeding into hard contractions. It is usually hours of hard contractions and the baby's head breaks the bag of waters when descending into the birth canal.

To help the mother go without medical intervention, the doctor will typically try manipulating the cervix first and give the mother a few extra days, as long as she is not past the 14 days. If manual manipulation has not worked and contractions have not begun, the doctor will ask you to check into the hospital so that the bag of water can be broken. If all the natural methods are exhausted and still no contractions, the doctor will insist on Pitocin because now the baby has no amniotic fluid protect it from infection. If Pitocin is administered, the contractions will be regular, INTENSE, and UNRELENTING.

Please keep this fact in mind; on D-Day your partner may go into the labor and delivery room full of courage and resolve, but childbirth is not easy, no matter the duration. Studies have shown that most women go into Active labor with the full intention of giving birth without medication. But at some point, their tenacity diminishes, and they end up having medicated births[i]. Of these women, 61% will have an epidural and will be physically numb to the experience. Most will have a vaginal delivery, but the others will end up having a C-section because the epidural or other medications may have stopped the body's natural process. Because there are no natural pain medication substitutes that can be used in a hospital, the only other option she has is for you to be her Daddy Doula. You will use the techniques from this book to reduce her pain when you can and give her the encouragement, she needs to make it through the labor one contraction at a time. I wonder how many of the women who choose a medicated route would have chosen differently if their partner was a Daddy Duala? I bet in the future; we will see the number of C-sections going down because of men like you who are reading this book.

Chapter 5:
Becoming a Daddy Doula - Creating the Trust and the Connection

If you have picked up this book in the hopes of being able to support your partner during the birth of your baby, you will find in this book all the methods and techniques required to be a useful contributor during the pregnancy and for L&D. But I don't want you to be just a "useful contributor" to your partner. I want you to be connected to her and be a part of the experience. For some of us, the connection is where the work is required. I know it was for me, and we were married!

When you are married, especially newly married, you may automatically assume that you have this deep connection with your partner and that your love will carry you through every situation. For the most part I think that when marriage is worked on, your love can get you through most marriage trials and tribulations. But to be a woman's partner in childbirth, it will require a different mindset and a different kind of connection. For the woman, she is literally carrying all the weight and enduring all the pain from beginning to end. The man cannot take up a traditional role of being the muscle or creating a solution to the problem. For this situation there is literally no way for you to lighten the load or take away the pain. You must accept that you are secondary and that you are there solely for support and encouragement. You must be the emotional rock that she can lean on, or a reassuring shoulder to cuddle with when needed. You must have an endless source of patience, assurance and recognition. But what your partner mostly needs from you is your capacity to reinforce her abilities and mental fortitude so that she will have the confidence she can endure the labor to the end.

Question: So how do we get you to that point where you have the unyielding trust of your partner and can help her bring your baby into the world?

Answer: By connecting yourself to the pregnancy and her.

The good news is you should have between 6 and 8 months after the great reveal, depending on when you found out about the pregnancy, to get you and your partner intertwined like a tightly woven friendship bracelet. With the help of the next few sections you might even have a few specialty charms to add to the bracelet to show off.

Chapter 5.1:
Baby Projects

When you found out that your partner was pregnant, you were probably excited, and definitely a whole lot of scared. With your back straight, chest out, and arms flexed, you were ready to do all that "guy stuff" that has been ingrained into your subconscious to get ready for the baby. You were instantly ready to wake up at 3 A.M. and purchase exotic food combinations of pickles with caramel ice cream, jalapenos with peanut butter, and boxes of mangos. You probably also remembered you owned a hand-me-down skill saw and decided that it was time to fix that creaky step. But mostly I bet you could see yourself walking behind that new lawn mower cutting parallel lines into the yard and swinging that weed-wacker shaping those extras dense "flower beds" into your personal botanical garden for all the future visitors to gawk over when walking up to the front door with baskets of little goodies for the new baby. The good news, I am glad you are excited to work hard to do all the above. The bad news, to be a Daddy Doula you have a lot more to do. Remember you are entering into a partnership. If you want to connect to the pregnancy you can't leave all things nursery, car-seat, baby clothes, and all the other "cute" stuff to her.

Before taking on the Daddy Doula challenge, I was the super stoked lawn guy with the 80's headband and extra-large safety goggles.

For my first girl, in the first trimester I chose to take on the typical male role and was really only concerned about the house, yard, and running errands. In all my excitement, after one good weekend of hard work outside in the summer sun, I had knocked out the yard work. The next weekend I repaired the loose cabinets, changed all the blown light bulbs, and replaced all batteries in the smoke detectors. I was generally done; now all I had to do was maintain my work until the baby was born. But after a few weeks of no new projects, I found myself without a mission. Because my wife is self-reliant, I quickly noticed she rarely called on me to run any errands nor was she ready to take on new home improvement projects. When it came to errands, I probably did myself a little disservice because when the call did come to go on to the grocery store, I got the new items requested but also doubled the stock of pickles, ice cream and mangos so my binge watching of the Walking Dead was interrupted as few times as possible. After the first big push of "man" chores, I found myself milling around while watching her midsection grow doing my normal routine. Mostly I found myself watching football and eating nachos with extra jalapenos while she was reading mom magazines and blogs, as well as talking to other friends who were new moms. She was fully engaged in the pregnancy and I was just emotionally investing in the prospects of my NFL team actually making the playoffs. One day, early into the second trimester, the universe provided me a choice. My wife wanted to go crib shopping at the mall and asked if I wanted to go with her or stay home to do laundry. At first, I thought about all the football games I was going to have to watch on the late-night highlight reels and how annoyed I was going to be after spending twenty minutes in the overcrowded consumer hell called the mall. But for some reason in the depths of my sole a gremlin kicked the frontal lobe of my brain, and I grumpily accepted her offer. Much to my surprise, I really enjoyed it. Whoever would have thought there were so many types of cribs to choose from in the world: cribs that are banned by the US Consumer Product Safety Commissions, cribs that transform into toddler beds, and cribs that vibrate like a car. Prior to our mall outing, my wife had already done most of the research on cribs. Before she made the purchase, she wanted to go to a few stores to put her hands on the cribs, as well as help me get an understanding of styles and costs. By the end of the day we agreed on style, color, and budget. To satiate my cheapness, we also decided we were going to purchase the crib and other nursery items on Black Friday when the deals were extra sweet. Now with the corner stone furniture piece of the nursery selected, my wife began to create her vision of the quick comfortable retreat for our new baby. I believe my wife sensed a new excitement and initiative in me. I was interested in preparing for the baby and began involving me with other nursery decisions. The Grumpalumpagus in me was saying that I should help out with the nursery to make sure we stayed on budget. The sprouting Daddy Doula in me was saying to jump in open hearted and be a part of the moment. No matter which alter ego showed up, we began discussing together the different themes and colors of the room depending on if it was a boy or a girl. There was compromise here and there. At first, we had to work a boy and a girl theme because the gender was still not known. If it was a boy, we had to decide between a Star Wars motif with a model Death Star, Millennium Falcon suspended from the corner of the room, and stuffed Yodas and Jabas: or a Barn Yard motif with wooden crates mounted to the wall to simulate the barn door and lots of stuffed animals. Can you pick my vision of the nursery? Thankfully we never had to make this decision, or have this argument over cows versus Imperial Walkers, because in the middle of our decorating strategy sessions we found out we were having a girl. I did not have much creative input on a girl's room except that I did not want Pink to be the primary color. FYI. If you were wondering when in the timeline the Doula conversation occurred, it was soon after the gender reveal. I wonder if that had anything to do with the fact, we were having a girl?

Child Proofing the Home

There is only one child proof house and that is a house without a child. But since you have one coming into your world, it is best that you bind, secure, fill, and lock up as much as you can to save yourself a lot of stress and potential heartache. Child proofing the house has a little expense involved, but mostly a time commitment. The good news is some smart people have invented lots of tools to help you in the childproofing process and nature has given you the whole pregnancy to get prepared. If you are not ready by the time the child is crawling, you are going to be scrambling around like Two Stooges with a hammer and broom building and cleaning at the same time.

There are a few general rules that I believe you will find to be beneficial in all rooms:

- Minimize what can be viewed at 3 feet (in other words, grabbed)

- If it hangs, make sure it is earthquake proof

- If it can be pulled, strap it or lock it down

- If it can be penetrated, plug it

If you apply these simple rules when preparing your shopping list, you will quickly determine that your house is a death trap for kids. But not to worry, with some ingenuity you can make every room almost disaster free.

To get started, the first thing you must do is step back and imagine you are 2 feet tall and are hyper-curious about everything. Tell yourself nothing can hurt me because I do not know what the object of my eyes' desire tastes like, feels like, smells like, or even what it is named. I just want to grab it, lick it, poke it, roll with it, insert it, and give it to the dogs. I will want it even more if I see you playing with it, eating with it, looking at it, and giving it to the dogs.

The second thing you must do is get rid of your knick-knacks! This killed me. I have a collection of pencil sharpeners that look like canons, cars, clocks, etc. I think they are cool because each marks a point in history. Don't laugh! No matter how "cool", these items had to go into a box. If you are like my wife and I, we needed a real good excuse to consolidate, purge, and organize our house. Moving to Texas was one. Having a baby was another.

The next sections for Child Proofing Projects will focus on each room of the house one at a time and provide you with a few suggestions. You will get the gist of my approach and be able to add to the list quickly once you get going.

Kitchen Nightmares

The kitchen is probably the most dangerous room in the house, or at least has the most potential to be the most dangerous. There are kitchen utensils, chemicals, fire, food, and probably a few dozen other elements of danger. Each danger in the kitchen is unique in its own right and may require different solutions. The one thing going for you is that the kitchen is designed for storage. Most of our cookware and utensils are already secured behind cabinets and in drawers. The spatulas, filet knives, and other utensils you keep in that decorative cylinder by the stove will have to be transferred to a drawer or be hidden behind a cabinet until you cook. Below are some tools that I have discovered that are great for keeping curious hands out of danger zones.

Drawer and Cabinet Locks:

Drawer and Cabinet Locks are simple devices. The locks are relatively cheap and easy to install. Basically, the locks allow the cabinet to be opened a few inches before the lock engages. In these few inches, opposable thumbs become handy and can unlatch the lock. Fortunately, a child does not have the strength or intellect to master this skill until they are around 3. Hopefully by then they know knives are sharp and can hurt you. At least the child should know they are not allowed in the knife drawer. In our house, my wife set up one cabinet and one drawer that our daughters can open at any time. We keep our Tupperware in one cabinet and drawing paper, crayons, and some other soft like objects in one drawer. Over time the girls learned which drawer was theirs and seemed to lose interest in the others.

But don't get me wrong, there were some strong NOs enforced before the girls grasped the concept of the No Access Allowed in drawers and cabinets. We also found that the locks did their jobs. They stopped and frustrated our girls just long enough for my wife or me to realize they were in the danger zone and were able to remove them from the situation.

Cleaning = Chemicals = Poison

Underneath just about every kitchen sink is a plethora of cleaning products. The typical montage under every sink are counter cleaners, glass cleaners, dust cleaners, stove cleaners, and of course the rags and brushes used for the cleaning. In this one spot, there are more dangerous items to you and your kids than in any other part of the house. Some of these products can blind, burn, and even kill a young child if they are swallowed, inhaled, or if it comes into contact with the skin. If there is one cabinet that needs to be secured, it is the kitchen sink cabinet. I would suggest a more difficult cabinet lock that requires a knob to be turned. This style of lock takes some thought to unlatch and will not accidently come unlocked if your little Hercules decides to apply some of his or her might. But you do have to remember to put it back on once you are done because it will not lock itself.

Beyond locking the cabinets, there is one thing you can do to make yourself ready in case there is some crazy accident and your child swallows some cleaner or it spills on them while you are cleaning. You can create an MSDS book for your kitchen. What is an MSDS book? Material Safety Data Sheet, MSDS. Get a good inventory of the name brands of all your cleaners and go to this website www.msds.com. You can search for your products and print out the MSDS data sheet. The data sheet will tell you what is in the product and how to handle the initial first aid response such as rinsing eyes or inducing vomiting. I would suggest creating a little binder and hang it on the inside of the cabinet to be ready at all times. On the front you can put contact information for Poison Control.

American Association of Poison Control Centers

1 (800) 222-1222

Hours: 24 hours, 7 days a week

Languages: English

Website: www.aapcc.org

You can get creative with the binder. Make a skull and cross bones for the cover or whatever you might do to make it scary. As your kids get older you can teach them how to use the book in the event one of the baby sibling gets splashed with bleach when they are doing a surprise cleaning for mom while she is at the store.

There is another alternative. You could use Bio Green Clean. Basically, with Bio Green Clean you have a one stop shop for all household cleaning products. You can discard, or donate to a local shelter, all of those toxic cleaning products and substitute one extraordinary cleaner. According to its MSDS worksheet, Bio Green Clean is a very environmentally and child friendly product. It is the only cleaner I know of that can clean a blackened oven, make your car tires shine, and remove stains from your clothes that will not hurt you or your child if it is ingested, bathed in, or smelled. I have been using the product for over 8 years and still I am amazed at what it can do. Go to www.biogreenclean.com and get all of your cleaning product needs in one product. (Free Endorsement!)

Beyond the cabinet locks, I would also add the following to your kitchen repertoire:

- ABC Fire Extinguisher – Used on electric, chemical, or normal fires.
- CO2 Monitor especially if you have gas stoves, ovens, or furnaces.

Since we are talking kitchen, I might as well bring up Safe Cooking Tips. As a general practice when cooking on the stove or with the oven, follow these rules:

1. Kids are not allowed by the stove or the oven when mommy and daddy are cooking. This is one of the most important rules of the kitchen until the child is at least 13 or 14 and can cook for themselves. Go visit a children's burn unit if you want to know what can happen in an unmeasurable second to a child that pulls down a hot pot of chili or a hot skillet of cooking grease.

2. All hot liquids go on the back burners.

3. All handles are turned to the back or at least away from the edge to prevent little Johnnie from practicing his Parkour routine when he comes screaming through the

kitchen

4. Before you remove anything from the stove or oven, make sure all kids are out of the kitchen or in their highchairs. Also, don't be a hero and use mitts when you are grabbing anything hot. It is double whammy when you grab that handle that you think is not hot or the hot water tips out of the pot onto your hand:

Whammy 1 - burned hand.

Whammy 2 - a very dirty kitchen.

Over the next few months start practicing 2, 3 and 4. By the time the child arrives, these safe kitchen practices will be second nature.

Kitchen Appliances:

As far as appliances go, there are really no inherent risks to them as long as they are not running. So, before you turn on your dishwasher or dryer, just make sure no one is taking a nap inside.

Bathrooms

Your bathrooms are similar to kitchens when it comes to cleaning chemicals. If you must keep them located under the bathroom sink, follow the same principles above and add the cabinet stops. But I would just transfer all the cleaning supplies to one cabinet and lock it down.

Probably the biggest danger in the bathroom are your medications. Pain relievers, cough suppressants, sleeping aids, and all other over-the-counter drugs, can cause severe health issues to your child if one is ingested. I suggest gathering all these drugstore medications, as well as your prescriptions, and place them in plastic box with a locking lid. Then place the medicine box on a top shelf in the linen closet. You will have to be diligent about returning it to the closet, but at least the locking top will give some additional security to the medicines in case you leave it out when in a hurry.

Unfortunately, the age to stop the practice of locking up drugs never comes. So many children steal parents' drugs and may even sell them to other children. You must be diligent and safe with drugs in your house.

Bedrooms

There typically are not many chemicals kept in a bedroom, but the furniture is an innocuous jungle gym of danger for babies to climb on, fall off of, and overturn onto them. Here are a few tips to help alleviate some of the dangers of furniture and decorations:

1. Use D-hooks and straps to secure chest of drawers to the wall.

2. Use Screws with square backs to hang pictures to provide a lip to hold the wire or anchor. This type of screw will help prevent slipping when walls are being banged. In addition, use sheetrock mollies no matter how light the items being hung.

3. Use wide based end-tables to hold lamps. If you can press down on it with two fingers and it starts to tip, it should probably not be in the room.

4. Make sure all cords for blinds or curtains are bound together and are not within reaching distance.

5. Do not leave your infant lying on the bed unsupervised. The day you think the baby can't roll over or scoot itself is the day the baby takes a head dive off the bed.

Living Rooms

Most of the dangers in the living room are the decorations and the floors. I would do the following:

1. Remove framed Pictures or other knick-knacks from all end-tables.

2. Move all items that can be grabbed to above 4 ft. Usually the mantle and top shelves are your best bet

3. If you have tiled or hardwoods, make sure there is a rug at the base of all couches and chairs. In the event the child does fall off, at least they will have a softer landing. Just don't leave baby unattended on a bed or other furniture.

4. If you have stairs, add a baby gate to the top and bottom. Once that little baby gets to crawling, it will become a great adventurer. The stairs will be the first test of bravery. Imagine the baby made it halfway up and sees you. With a big smile and wave, baby loses balance and tumbles all the way back down to the base with a bang.

5. If you live where there are fireplaces, and they are actually used, then safety screens should always be in place.

6. If you have floor heating or wood fired stoves, wood or metal barricades like dog gates are your best bet. Plastic

might melt.

7. If you have indoor plants, then I would check to see if the leaves or flowers are poisonous. If so, they should be donated to the neighbor or the local retirement home. Here is a list of a few:

    - Philodendron

    - Pothos

    - Arrowhead

    - Lily

    - Peace Lily

    - Dieffenbachia

    - Oleander

Outdoor Areas

Other than the obvious spiders, snakes, raccoons, and bears that love to be outside when your kids are playing, there are a few other items you should look into if you plan on introducing your little explorer to the beauties of nature.

1. Identify the plants in your yard. Poison Ivy and Oak can be nasty plants if you decide to have a tickle party in them.

2. Store all yard tools, fertilizers, and other lawn treatments in a locked shed. You can also create a MSDS book for lawn chemicals.

3. Do not cut the grass with your kid sitting on the porch playing GI Joe Saves the Day. I know this might seem silly, but unless you literally comb your yard before you start cutting, you never know what is hiding deep in the weeds. What if Snake-Eyes was on a reconnaissance mission in the jungle when you encounter him with your bushwhacker and the mower throws his severed head right through your plate glass window, or your kid's eye.

4. Disconnect your grill from the gas after every use. That little gas nob is easy to turn for curious hands. What if your little Dora was playing with the grill thinking she was throttling her rocket ship and created a slight gas leak? The gas builds up under the grill hood and when you light that 4th of July stogie a few hours later you get an

unexpected show.

5.   Similar to cooking in the kitchen, when grilling, no kids allowed within 5 feet of the fire.

All this safety might seem like overkill and like the mentality of those hovering helicopter parents. But actually, it is quite the opposite. By installing these safety controls, you are creating a safe environment for your baby to explore with less oversight. You have eliminated the hazard or have engineered a control to limit the risk to a known hazard. I am not suggesting that you go to the gym for a quick burn leaving the baby alone inside for an hour. But if your house is set up with proper safety measures, you can leave the living area to visit your throne room for a few minutes while your baby plays on the ground without worry about a lamp being pulled of a table and cracking the baby's head open.

My wife really likes me when I do errands or projects without much prodding and verbal repetition. She adores me when I sacrificed a little of my "Game Time" for some "Baby time". So, moral to the entire Baby Projects story, do all the projects with a smile and in advance of her schedule. I was a hit or miss on the Baby Project lesson for the first daughter that caused some unneeded stress. In the end the projects were completed in time to meet her schedule. (Note: there is typically a reason for the deadline she sets. For my wife, the project end date coincided with a baby shower. The baby shower was an opportunity to show off the nursery to her girlfriends and family. It was also the actual pressure point of all the stress). The night before the baby shower we walked through our little house reviewing all the work we had put in to making the house a home. From adding flowers and mulch to the beds outside, to hanging new ceiling fans with automatic light switches, to installing my wife's custom art, we were proud of ourselves. All the earlier arguments about color, lanterns, or watching too much football began to fade to relief and joy. The anticipation of the memories that were going to be created in our home outshined all the previous negative moments. The look in my wife's eyes that night told me I was a little more in tune with her and the pregnancy. I would highly recommend your full participation in the baby projects to help your connection to the pregnancy grow quicker and with less stress. There is no need to fight battles that you cannot win. Instead, if you are more agreeable and committed to working with her, you can actually end up creating other amazing moments in your story.

Chapter 5.2:
Picking the OBGYN

Not all Doctors are created equal. That would be my assessment based on personal experiences. From general health care visits, to sport related surgeries, and to a simple case of poison ivy, I have personally had the best and the quirkiest doctors; and OBGYN doctors are no different. They are all well trained at delivering babies. Each is capable of observing changes in the birth process. Each can assess conditions that are endangering the baby or the mother. And, each will deploy their skills to ensure a successful delivery. Assuming you have two very skilled doctors to choose from, there is one trait that you may find that will distinguish them from each other: their philosophy of birthing. Basically, is the doctor's philosophy going to be promoting a vaginal un-medicated birth from the beginning, or at the earliest challenge will they start pushing for medical interventions? The good news is that the OBGYN will be able to determine what type of birth is possible early on in pregnancy, i.e. virginal or C-section. Your partner will have a general physical and blood panel to see if there are any medical issues with her before D-Day. If there are issues, the OBGYN will start game planning with your partner prescribing medications for things like incompatible blood types, exercises to increase strength, etc. The doctor might even prescribe a C-Section from the beginning to ensure a healthy baby and mother. If there are medical issues, your birth plan will be already worked out with doctors and the medical team. But if your partner is healthy and there are no medical reasons for a C-section, then the OBGYN's philosophy will make a difference in the D-Day experience.

Indulge my sports analogy but hopefully this will help make it clear why the doctors birthing philosophy matters.

It is D-Day and you have just checked into the hospital for the delivery. At that moment, the nursing staff instantly becomes a part of your birthing team. The wife is the quarterback, you are the running back, and the nurses are the O-line. The doctor is the coach. Everyone on the team is provided the play sheet (i.e. the birth plan) that has been practiced by you and your partner and crafted with your doctor. The nurses know the primary doctor, so after a quick review of the plan by the nurses, the team philosophy is established, and everyone starts doing their part to ensure the game plan is successful. Here are a few observations I made about the nurses during my D-Day experiences to help you understand their role in the plan:

Observation 1: The nurses are trained to care for your partner and make her comfortable and safe.

Observation 2: The nurses are monitoring and caring for the mother until either something goes wrong and the doctor is needed to intervene in the birth process, or it is time to push.

Observation 3: The nurses work with different doctors and will do what it takes to make sure the doctor on duty is successful in delivering the baby.

Back to the analogy. It has been a few hours since you checked in and you both are playing a great game. The nurses are encouraging her along and Daddy Doula skills are being fully deployed. About 12 hours in, there is an expected shift change to the night staff. During the shift change we also find out our OBGYN is no longer available for the labor and delivery if it occurs in the next 4 hours. We would have to use the night shift OBGYN. The play sheet is passed out again to the nurses and the doctor. But this time instead of getting encouragement, the nurses start asking partner if she wants "Total Relief". The doctor believes that adding some Pitocin would speed things up but suggest that an epidural be administered to relieve the pain so she can relax. Suddenly, the quarterback is frazzled because up to this point there have been no indications that the current game plan was not working. Now she had plays coming from the sidelines for the 2-minute "come from behind" section of the playset. The O-line is following the lead of the Coach and the Running back is being benched.

Well that is about where the analogy ends without getting too convoluted. But you get the point. Simply put, the doctor sets the game plan. If the doctor prefers to get the mother on an epidural to keep the halls quiet of those Hollywood cries of pain, all he has to do is instruct the nurses to start pushing the new game plan.

But if the doctor prefers the natural process, the game plan will not change when things get hard, but make sure the team is still playing with the same philosophy. But most importantly, the nurses will be supportive, encouraging, and proactive like a Pro-Bowl O-line that takes all the great quarterbacks to a Big Game Victory.

So how can I get you more connected to the pregnancy and help you in the doctor selection process simultaneously? By providing you well thought out questions about L&D to ask during the doctor's interview. If you have been living in an area for a while, most likely your partner will already have an OBGYN for her general checkups. If not, she will have to select one quickly. In either case, she will want to make sure that the OBGYN is on board with an unmedicated vaginal delivery from the beginning. There is also a very good chance that you will not be attending the actual visits, so like all daddy doula's activities this one will require that you and your partner have a deep conversation and build your approach to the OBGYN. Below is a list of questions to help start the conversation that you can possibly ask the OBGYN.

1. Out of all the babies delivered in the last 4 weeks, what percent were through vaginal birth, with limited intervention? (I would bet the doctor will know exactly because it is rare these days)

2. What percentage of the deliveries in the last 4 weeks was the woman medicated with an epidural or other pain medications? Or if the data is not available, then ask in what situation will the Doctor suggest using an epidural or pain medications?

3. How does the doctor and staff encourage an unmedicated vaginal birth? Does the doctor or hospital have recommended literature or classes?

4. Who is the backup doctor in case the baby comes on the doctor's off day? Is the backup doctor's philosophy similar as the primary doctor? Can both of you meet the backup doctor over the next few months during one of the scheduled visits?

I am sure you can think of a few more probing questions that can help you evaluate the doctor. In my opinion, the doctor is paramount to a successful unmedicated vaginal birth because the mother can be reassured of the doctor's capabilities, while the doctor is ensuring the baby and the mother's health. Without preexisting medical issues or physical limitations as factors in the birth process, there really is no reason not to go vaginal. Even if your partner 's health is not an issue, please try to have some empathy no matter the positive potential. It still takes unbelievable amounts of courage, determination, and resilience by your partner to be successful at a unmedicated vaginal delivery, and of course a Daddy Doula's unyielding support.

Chapter 5.3:
Choosing the Hospital

You might be thinking after doing all the Baby Projects and selecting the doctor you would have a good connection with your partner, and well on your way to becoming a Daddy Doula. Not quite. As of right now you are your partner's "go-to handyman"; now it is time to get connected with the medical side of labor and delivery.

Life has a funny way of getting complicated fast. For months, I had been splashing my resume on the internet looking for new opportunities for engineering positions outside of Georgia. Ever since we got married, we had been talking about moving from the Atlanta area to Houston to get closer to my wife's parents. Because of the oil and gas boom in the US, there were lots of opportunities for engineers in the Lone Star State. My chances were better in Texas than most other states considering the sluggish economy and the State's Budget for infrastructure in 2011.

About two weeks into getting comfortable with the idea of being a father and raising our baby in a two-bedroom condo, I got a call from a good company in Houston for a position. In short, about a month after that phone call, we packed up our lives in Atlanta and started a new life in Houston. The job was exciting because of all the possibilities for my career, but for our family it was a little extra nerve racking. We were moving to a new city where we did not know many people. We did not have a clue about the quality of doctors and knew nothing about the hospitals that were in Houston.

My wife did some networking with some of her old Texas girlfriends who had children and got a few recommendations on Hospitals. Because we were in a major city like Houston and my company's insurance coverage was expansive, we had lots to choose from. Her search eventually directed us to the Texas Children's Hospital – Woman's Pavilion. We were lucky in the fact that this hospital focused solely on L&D. Because the hospital offered specific resources around L&D, and its staff dealt exclusively with mothers, we were able to have a great experience with our girls that I wish all of you can experience. (I will go into detail about the resources later in this section.)

Let me step back a little bit before we go into choosing your hospital. First, I understand that I am lucky to live in a city like Houston with such a unique hospital and your city or town might not have anything close to Texas Children. I understand that facilities across the country will very in quality and scope of services. Health Insurance is almost a taboo word, and there are many people out there who either do not have health insurance, employers only provide catastrophic coverage, or you pay for it off the exchanges. I do not want to go into Health Insurance coverage in too much detail, but a little extra information cannot be bad for a Daddy Doula.

Under the Affordable Car Act (Obamacare) your baby's Mom's Maternity coverage must be covered by all health insurance plans offered to individuals and families.

Per the law, the items below should not have any copay and are completely covered by the plan:

1.   Outpatient services, such as prenatal and postnatal doctor visits, gestational diabetes screenings, lab studies, and pregnancy medications

2.   Newborn baby care and check ups

3.   Lactation counseling and breast pump rental

The items below will have copay, or the cost will be applied to your deductible:

1.   Inpatient services, such as hospitalization for the labor and delivery

2.   C-section surgery

3.   Pitocin and anesthesia

4.   Other medication used during stay

5.   Other services used during stay.

See your HR Policy Manual for employer provided plans or www.heathcare.gov for personal insurance plans purchased on the market. The basic levels of coverage should match! The limit of the deductibles will determine the overall cost. There are a few adders like in-out of network benefits and prescription drug coverage that can also add cost.

Also check the policy to verify if the newborn will be insured. This is especially important, and often overlooked, because sometimes the coverage does not kick-in for 30 days. Should the newborn need extra health care after birth, the added cost may not be covered by your plan. Most of the time any post birth issues will be known and can be planned for with doctor and insurance companies.

If you have insurance, the easiest action to determine your L&D expenses is to contact your insurance provider. The representative will give you a breakout of all the expected costs based on your plan. If you have a low deductible plan, you should budget on spending between $200 and $1000 for services during pregnancy (neonatal) and the Labor and Delivery. If you have a high deductible plan or no insurance you, should budget for L&D costs of $3000 for vaginal delivery and $5000 for C-section. If you include neonatal services add $4000 to the total experience. (InsuranceCost)

No matter what insurance you have or what hospitals are available to you in your area, there is no reason for you not to have a great L&D experience. Except you and your mind set. Think about it this way. If your mind and heart are fully engaged in the moment, it will not matter where you give birth. Our ancient ancestors gave birth in caves and stables, so just about any hospital is a great L&D facility in comparison.

Now that the financial pain is out of the way, let's focus on making the Daddy Doula Connection. Selecting a Hospital should be done with your partner and selected by her. Remember this is her show and you are just along for the ride. If her girlfriend convinced her that Saint Bambino Hospital is a better L&D facility than Fred B. Kind Hospital, even though you think the scope of service is less, let it ride. It is not worth the fight. Just make sure the hospital is in your Insurance Network.

The easiest way to get your Daddy Doula mojo flowing when it comes to selecting a L&D Facilities is to do some research and identify all the facilities in your area. Note, not all hospitals will provide L&D services so you will need to call the facilities on your list to verify capabilities. The last thing you want to do is use an Emergency Room Services for the birth of your baby. The Emergency Room doctors can get the job done, and they might like to see life come into the world versus go out of the world on their shift, but it will not be cheap. To help you select the best L&D hospital for your area I will use our experiences at Texas Children's to establish a Gold Standard of services. With the high standard in place, it will be easy to rank your local hospital choices. Your hospital might not offer all these services, but at least when you are on your search, you can ask the right questions and maybe find outside resources to enhance the overall experience. To meet my Gold Standard for L&D Hospitals, the scopes of services should include at a minimum the following criteria as defined below.

GOLD STANDARD

1. Assessment Center

2. Private Labor and Delivery Rooms

3. Lactation Consultants

4. Recovery Room

If your L&D facility meets the Gold Standard, then you will have all the resources needed for a great experience. You might get lucky and the hospital you select will provide post L&D massages for you and your partner! But don't count on your insurance paying for it.

In the next few sections I will define each of the scopes of service of my Gold Standard. I will provide you insights from my own experiences that will demonstrate the benefits of the service and allow you to expand your list of services to include amenities like bathtubs, shower, stereos, and tv's. With the information provided, you both can apply the standard to your available choices to make the best decision.

Assessment Center

The Assessment Center is a part of the hospital or L&D facility that the expecting mother can go to have the baby and herself checked at any time if the mother is feeling there is something off with the pregnancy. This is not an emergency room for expecting mothers, but there will be an OBGYN and nurses there to check on your partner. This service is offered outside of the scheduled pre-natal visits. For instance, if the baby has not kicked in a while or your partner is having severe cramping, the Assessment Center is a good place to go for a quick diagnosis of the situation. We used this option a couple of times the last week of the pregnancies. Basically, when you go into the center, the nurse hooks the mother up to a contraction monitor and a fetal heart rate monitor to observe. Over an hour's time they monitor the baby's heart rate for signs of stress and determine if the uterus is contracting. The doctor will perform an ultrasound to make sure that the baby is not in a stressful position or if it has moved down into the birth canal. For our first daughter, my wife was not sure if she was feeling contractions or just having cramps due to gas from something she ate. It is easy to mistake contractions with bad gas. One night around week 35 my wife swore she was going into labor. I was rubbing her belly trying to sooth her. I found this really hard spot on the side of her stomach. I asked if it was the baby. She moved my hand further to the center where I could feel the baby's bottom. Out of curiosity, I moved my hand back to the hard spot and gave it gentle push without warning my wife. It was like hitting a real organic woopy cushion. But this one came with a ferocious odor. My action ended the false contractions and started a rally of gut-wrenching laughter.

A few days later my wife was performing her routine kick counts and the count was low. Kick Counts are a practice your partner will do to self-monitor the baby in the later stages of the pregnancy. Per the doctors' orders when the counts are low or can't be felt, she took a shower and drank some orange juice. After 10 minutes the kicks were still nonexistent. My wife's anxiety started to increase so we decided to go to the Assessment Center for some piece of mind. On this trip the doctor's tests revealed that all was well with the baby and nothing was really happening as far as contractions. The baby was just sleeping. I saw the worry leave my wife's eyes when she heard the heartbeat on the monitor.

Later that week we went back to the assessment center. It was also in the middle of the night. This time things had changed. The baby was great, but the contractions were real and early labor had started. They sent us home because she had not progressed beyond 2/90/-4 yet. This visit gave us the reassurance that what she was feeling was normal and the beginning of labor. Now we just had to wait for the L&D Dance to begin.

I highly recommend the hospital you choose provide the Assessment Center as part of the scope of services. The service was offered as part of the care provided by our chosen hospital and did not add additional prenatal care costs. I believe the hospital provided this service not only as a marketing tool, but I imagine it also can save money in the overall cost of care if situations are caught earlier rather than becoming emergencies. The Assessment Center provided my wife a major sense of security to know that she could go at any time to check on the baby. A secondary benefit to the service was that in the worst-case scenario, if you went in and the baby was stressed, the doctors and staff are there ready to deal with the situation. You might go in thinking you are there for checkup and end up with a baby in your arms a few hours later.

The Labor and Delivery Room

One of the essential characteristics to look for in the hospital or L&D Facility you are going to be delivering your baby is the type of L&D Room. The L&D Room played a major role in my wife's ability to go through labor naturally and without being embarrassed by her loud moans. The room that the Women's Pavilion provided was private to only the staff and me. It was designed to set up a relaxing environment for the mother with tools to be utilized during active and transition labor.

It is probably hard to imagine a room in a hospital being relaxing, much less an L&D room. I am sure a few movies have corrupted your imagination into thinking that there is this bed that resembles a torture table made to restrain a mad-woman with foot and wrist stirrups. I love movies and how they stir our imagination, but most rooms are just normal hospital beds. There are foot stirrups, but they are used in the transition stage when the baby is being delivered to give the mother some grip for pushing. I am assuming here your partner chooses to lay on her back instead of kneeling on all fours or some other position that suites her in the moment. Yes, there is more than one way to deliver the baby. There are more important characteristics to the room to consider other than the bed. Below is my essential list that makes it on the Gold Standard:

Private L&D Room

Not all hospitals have the "bed" space to ensure each mother has her own private room. Sometimes the room can be shared with another mother with only a curtain separating the two beds. I would strongly suggest a private room, especially if you are going vaginal with no medication. If your choice is limited to the dorm like delivery room, I would encourage you to get to know the other family and make it a team effort. It is all about the village. Plus, with your Daddy Doula training, you might be able to get two babies into the world without medication.

Walking Space

There will always be hallways in a hospital, but those are less private. Space is the key to your sanity and for the two of you to work your doula moves. If your partner is on medication, the medical staff will not let her move around, so space is not much of an issue. For our deliveries we walked miles of hospital halls, slow danced, walked around in tiny circles, did squatting routines, and even crawled a little.

Jacuzzi Tub

The tub feature bought us about 2 hours of no epidural with the first two deliveries. We typically found ourselves in the heated tub with jets streaming onto her back and me using the shower wand to warm her head. At the very end when the contractions were the hardest and longest, the tub seemed to provide an extra element of relief once the contraction subsided. If this feature is not available, then I would plan on using hot wash clothes soaked in lavender oil to rub her back. Ask the nurse if they have heated blankets or towels as well.

Stereo System

A stereo with a docking station for your phone or other music device will change the mood of a room from a quiet asylum to a calm sanctuary. If the docking station is not available, most rooms have a wand that is used to communicate with the nurse's stand that also controls the volume from the TV or radio. We had the wand. It played Pandora from a small computer hooked to the TV in the room, but the sound was of poor quality. I made sure for the second baby that I brought an external speaker that played music from my phone. Trust me you will need something to pass the time. Music is a good way to fill the silence with some relaxing tunes. You might find yourself listening to the greatest song of all time when the head crowns. Pearl Jam's "Daughter" was ironically on when my second was born. (No Joke!!)

Recovery Room

After the birth of your little baby vaginally or by other means, the mother is going to need to begin her healing process. A recovery room should almost be a little hotel room. At the minimum I would expect in a semi-modern hospital there should be appurtenance like TV, radio, and a full bathroom. Once you go beyond those basic features, the recovery room is taking on extra benefits that are geared to make you and your partner more comfortable during the stay. To keep with the theme of creating a Gold Standard, for Recovery Rooms the list of appurtenances below will make your stay more relaxing and enjoyable. If the L&D room and the Recovery Room are the same room, then the list below should be added to the detail of the L&D room.

1. Cable TV and Netflix
2. Docking station for music
3. 2-in-1 Couch. This feature will serve as sitting area during visiting hours and a bed for you at night. However, don't expect it to be soft like silk and plush like a pillow.
4. Recliner that rocks. This can be used by you while you read your favorite book while waiting to change the next diaper. It can also be used by your partner when she wants to breast feed or just get out of the bed.
5. Privacy Partition between the room door and the bed. This will prevent curious eyes from peering into the private moments of your room as they pass by the door

while walking the halls.

6. Closet Space to hang cloths. It is nice to unpack your bags and get your cloths organized for the hospital stay.

7. Dinner table so that you both can eat meals together, versus you in the recliner and her in the bed. Some hospitals will have some versatile rollaway tables that are made to fit over the hospital bed or can be expanded to make a two-person table.

8. Shelves to store gifts and flowers. This will minimize the clutter in the room that can eat up precious space.

9. A 5 to 7 feet U shaped path between the bed and any other furniture in the room. This will allow a space for visitors to stand without crowding the bed and for an area for the mom to walk with the baby in the privacy of the room.

I am sure there are L&D hospitals that will go Platinum when it comes to comfort as long as you or your insurance is willing to pay for it. Generally, when it comes to a comfortable Recovery Room, I would look for features that promote privacy, rest, and space.

No matter how much you try to minimize the commotion In the room there always will be nursing staff checking on mom and baby, hospital administrators gathering paperwork, and pediatric doctors coming to give their blessing. Along with the hospital personnel there is also an uprising of family members and friends who want to visit so they can lay their germ covered hands on your soft little dumplin'. With all the people moving in and out of the room it is important to ensure the hospital and the room has a security system in place. That system should have the following characteristics:

1. Security Guard with an ID check-in point. The guard can check the ID against a supplied guest list to ensure your estranged uncle doesn't crash the party.

2. Baby Check In/Out Procedures. This Recovery Room feature is a system designed to prevent the occurrence of a kidnapping. Hospitals will use wrist bands with pertinent information to match mother to baby and father to baby. Once you and your partner check into the hospital you will be given an ID bracelet. Once the baby is born, the baby will be given an ID bracelet that has matching information on it. The bracelets are used as a cross-reference system. For instance, if the baby must leave the room for a checkup the staff must sign-off on a checkout form with the mother or approved representative. Once the baby is brought back into the room the wrist bands and the signed document are matched. Some hospitals will have systems that if a bracelet is cut or if it crosses a certain point in the hospital the bracelet will signal an alarm and lock all exits. The check in/out procedure will ensure the mother or father are always aware of the location of the baby to reduce any unneeded stress. It will also make sure the

correct baby leaves the hospital with the rightful mother.

The keys to a Recovery Room are comfort and security. In a strong free-market of recovery rooms, the local L&D hospitals will most likely go a little out of their way to make sure that you and your partner have a good experience. So, if all other hospital choices are equivalent, let the recovery room be the deciding factor because the end of your experience will make a lasting impression.

Lactation Consultant

Some hospitals and L&D facilities have trained nurses on staff that specialize in breast feeding that are generally referred to as a Lactation Consultant (LC). A Gold Standard Facility will provide an LC as part of the general care of L&D. If an LC in not available in any of the hospitals or L&D facilities in your area, your OBGYN will be your next best option. The doctor will either be very familiar with breast feeding or can refer you to someone in the area you can contact; such as the La Leche League (https://www.llli.org).

So why does it matter if the facility offers a LC? Baby Food. One of the most important parts of ensuring a healthy and happy baby after delivery is good eating. There are two good ways to provide your new baby the needed nutrients, formula or breast milk. The LC can provide your partner guidance on different methods on how to get the baby to latch onto the nipple and what to expect when it comes to overall feeding routines. If breast feeding is difficult in the beginning, the LC can teach Mom how to use the breast pump to stimulate or control milk production.

Since we are talking about breast feeding, it is a good time to throw a little information into the mix about breast milk. Nursing the baby with breast milk provides many benefits for the newborn:

1. Antibodies - the mother develops antibodies with her own immune system and the defense system is transferred to the baby during feedings. For example, the

baby's tear duct can get clogged and will get a minor infection. Apply a little breast milk to the duct and the infection will most likely clear up.

2.   Nutrients – Milk without fat, vitamin and mineral nutrients is just water. The mother's body will pull from sources like bone marrow and stored fat to create a well-balanced meal for your newborn. Because her body is using its own stores to make the milk it is very important that she is eating well balanced meals!

For first time mothers, breast feeding might seem like a formidable task, and possibly frustrating if the milk is having a hard time generating. When your partner can't do it on her own, that's when the LC can be a useful coach and when engineered formula can be substituted for the breast milk. If either of you become concerned about not being able to breast feed, do not worry. There is nothing wrong with using formula, but it is like coffee, some are better than others. And if formula is out of the question there are breast milk banks that you can purchase a supply. Yes, there are breast milk banks like there are blood banks. Unlike blood banks, breast milk banks are not really regulated so you arc not sure of the "health" of the milk. Even with all the options for alternative milk supplies, it is important to be patient when it comes to breast feeding. Some mothers take days or weeks to get their milk supply to enough volume to satisfy the nutritional needs of the baby. Until then, formula or bank milk will do the job of fattening up your little pork chop. Other than the nourishment side of breast feeding, my wife especially enjoys the feeding time for the connection and personal time she gets with the baby. The best advice when it comes to ensuring your baby gets enough food is to use the expertise of the LC to help you plan how to feed your new baby. Trust me the LC is worth the time because the better your baby feeds the better the baby sleeps. And the better the baby sleeps the more you are going to sleep.

Now, you have a general outline of what to look for in an L&D hospital. So, what do all engineers do once they know all the variables to the equation, they create a spreadsheet! Nothing says organized Daddy Doula like a spreadsheet of L&D Hospitals in your area. I want you to create an initial list that you can hand over to your partner for her review. Provide details like how long it will take to arrive from your house in rush hour traffic, as well as the scopes of services each offers. When you have your list complete, put it in a funny pregnancy card from the store and ask your partner out on a date. That's right; you are going to take her on a date to find a Hospital! Hand her the card and wait for the insane laughter. Once she stops laughing at your romantic skills, propose to her instead of doing projects this weekend you would like to take her to lunch and to find a L&D hospital she would like to use.

The hospital checklist she finds in the card might look something like this:

Hospital	Insurance	Commute	Assessment Center	Private Labor and Delivery Room	Lactation Consultants	Recovery Room
St. Bambino	√	1 hour	NA	√	√	√
Mike B. Kind	√	35 min.	√	NA	√	√

Boom! Instant Smile and all kinds of Daddy Douala connections being made!

Chapter 5.4:
Creating the Birth Plan

Now that you and your partner have picked out a doctor and hospital, it is time to pull all the L&D information together into a detailed birth plan. You might be asking why do you need a detailed birth plan? Answer. So that you always look like the smartest dad in the L&D building. A detailed understanding of L&D and having it on paper does two things: it demonstrates your complete understanding of the process and it significantly reduces the stress of D-Day by being proactive versus reactive to the birthing process.

Creating the birth plan is an activity that requires mostly your partner and the doctor's input. But what you can do to show off your Daddy Doula credentials is to provide a basic worksheet with details and questions to work from when creating the final form. The plan will coincide with the medical recommendations of the doctor. The most important component of the plan is to establish your goals with the medical team and for it to be used as the Play Sheet on D-Day. Below I will provide the birth plan sections and general information that should go on your Birth Plan. It will be up to the two of you to compose a complete plan. The plan should be broken into two sections: Home and Hospital. The sections will provide decision making points at each location and direct you to certain predetermined actions associated with the labor.

Birth Plan: Home

The Home Section of the birth plan should cover how you are going to approach the Pre-Labor phase. It should provide a strategy for contraction monitoring, eating, and hydration. Most importantly, it should detail how you are going to get your partner to the hospital once she transitions from Pre-Labor to Active Labor.

Contraction Monitoring – Eating and Drinking

Let's assume that your partner does not have one of those unicorn L&D stories and it actually takes at least 24 hours of Pre-Labor before active labor starts. To help track the progress of the labor you should keep a journal of the start, end, and duration of each contraction when they start becoming regular. As a Daddy Doula, you want to be very aware of the labor progress. Once labor is at the 5:1:2 contraction ratio (5 minutes apart, 1 minute long, 2-minute break), your Birth plan should activate the following activities:

1. Notifying family and work you are on your way to the hospital. These people should be identified on the plan with associated phone numbers and email addresses. This might seem silly but in all the excitement your phone could fall into a puddle or break on the way out the door. Unless you actually know phone numbers by heart, then the birth plan is your backup database.
2. Load the Go Bag. I have an entire section in this book that

describes the Go Bag. If you are inquisitive, it is okay to read Chapter 7.

3. Begin prepping the house for lock down for your 3-day vacation. Create a checklist of activities:

    - Stove Off.
    - Dishwasher Off.
    - Windows locked
    - Doors locked.

4. If you have pets, you should have a plan to have them cared for while you are away. They are resilient creatures that could probably survive 3 days with just toilet bowl water, but animals tend to make messes when cooped up without supervision and good loving.

The time it can take to go from Pre-Labor to Active labor can be long and will have both anxiety and excitement stirring in the pot. Because of all the emotions, and the pain of the contractions, your partner can forget to do essential tasks like scheduling meals and drinking fluids. Because you are her Daddy Doula, you will be there to ensure that during this period of time your partner is drinking and eating. Once she is checked into the L&D hospital, the only nourishment she will be provided are ice chips. Hospitals typically try to avoid the consumptions of solids and fluids when checked into the L&D room in the event an emergency surgery is needed. Choking becomes a serious hazard, and liability, when a contraction pushes her ribeye lunch special to the surface when she is under anesthesia. Good news is that what you eat and drink prior to the hospital taking responsibility of the patient is up to you. I would not suggest a ribeye but prefer protein bars or light meals to keep her nourished. There is no substitute for water to ensure hydration. The combination of the food and liquids will improve her overall endurance. I would suggest at least 4 oz. of water every 30 minutes and some sort of light protein every hour. I would also throw some fruit and sports drinks into the rotation to keep her performing at optimum condition. Like a supreme athlete prepping for the big game, the more food she has available to burn and the more hydrated she is during active labor, the more energy she will have to sustain her through the L&D. To help with the tracking of fluids and food, your Birth Plan can include a food and hydration log. But to knock out two birds with one stone we are going to create one log that will track the contraction progress along with the food and water. The log should look something like the one below.

Contraction Log						
Contraction	Start	Stop	Duration (Stop - Start)	Break	Drink	Eat
1	5:30:00 A.M.	5:30:30 A.M.	30 sec			
2	5:45:00 A.M.	5:45:45 A.M.	45 sec	15 minutes	yes	
3	6:00:00 A.M.	6:01:00 A.M.	60 sec	15 minutes		
4	6:15:00 A.M.	6:16:15 A.M.	75 sec	15 minutes	yes	
5	6:30:00 A.M.	6:31:30 A.M.	90 sec	15 minutes		
6	6:45:00 A.M.	6:46:45 A.M.	105 sec	15 minutes	yes	yes
7	7:00:00 A.M.	7:02:00 A.M.	120 sec	15 minutes		
8	7:15:00 A.M.	7:17:15 A.M.	135 sec	15 minutes	yes	
9	7:30:00 A.M.	7:32:30 A.M.	150 sec	15 minutes		
10	7:45:00 A.M.	7:47:45 A.M.	165 sec	15 minutes	yes	yes

There are some free apps out there that can help with calculations for contraction ratios. You can use the app for the timing, but I would log the results by hand. Not only does it make you active in the labor, it also creates a little story board to reflect on once the baby is here.

Commutes and Travel

When it comes to L&D, time is either your friend or your enemy. Sometimes an event can come too quick to comprehend and sometimes the event seemingly drags on for days. To help you plan for the unscheduled event of labor, the birth plan should identify the most likely places you and your partner could be when active labor starts. The locations will allow you to plan for overall drive times so that you can plan your trip to the L&D hospital. Here are a few scenarios to consider for your plan. You will have to determine the commute times. For all cases, check you traffic maps before you leave to make sure you have the best route.

Both of you are at Home together on weekend.

Traffic is typically minimal on the weekends so the commute should be straight forward. The two of you would go to the hospital when she hits the 2:1:1 contraction ratio or when the bag of waters breaks. If your city has major sporting events in your route to the hospital, then I would suggest knowing your teams schedule and having back up routes to bypass the stadiums.

You are at work and she is at work on opposite ends of town.

Rush Hour Traffic is possible so assume the commute is longer than normal. This scenario is a little more complicated. First you have to consider if you want to meet up at the house before going to the hospital or head straight to the hospital from work. (Decision Point) As long as you are not close to the 2:1:1 contraction ratio, you probably have a few hours to regroup and head out together from the house. But if for some crazy reason, your partner's bag of waters breaks, she will need to be at the hospital within an hour or two. (Decision Point). You will have to map out a trip from work to home then to the hospital to determine total time on the road. Similarly, you will have to map a trip from work to the hospital and determine total drive time. Compare the times to see which is fastest. If you have conversations about your commute regularly with a coworker, then I would assume that traffic is a nightmare in your area. You will need to make sure your plan for this scenario is well thought out. The plan might even require a Go Bag to be kept in both cars and you might have to employ some coworkers to assist in driving your partner to the hospital.

She is more than 3 hours out of town with or without you.

First, try your best to not book any trips in the last 4 weeks. But if your partner must make a road trip, she should carry the following information with her:

1. Birth Plan
2. General Health and Pregnancy Information. The doctor should be able to provide a packet. It should include any issues that the doctor and your partner are dealing with like high blood pressure, diabetes, depression, STD's, etc.

3. Location of L&D Hospital close to hotel or wherever she is staying. Your partner could even have your doctor reach out to the hospital to get the new OBGYN information for a quick consult. This is a better option than the Emergency Room, but if your partner goes into labor in a strange town, the emergency room will be her best bet.

Here is a quick table to illustrate the information:

Commute Table				
Hospital Name		Hospital Location:		Phone:
Location	Commute Home	Commute to Hospital	Meet at Home	Meet at Hospital
Home	--	45 minutes	--	--
Dad Work	45 minutes	55 minutes	yes	no
Mom Work	30 minutes	20 minutes	no	yes
Grandma's House	15 minutes	45 minutes	yes	no

I believe you can see where I am going with these location examples. In your plan, account for time in the best-case scenario, the worst-case scenario, and everything in between. The last thing you want to happen is that the baby is delivered by an EMT on the side of the road while you are stuck in bumper to bumper traffic just 2 miles away from the hospital. Come to think of it, if it is only a few miles, just pull over to the side of the road and just run for it. I can see the headlines now...

Birth Plan: Hospital

For the Hospital section of the birth plan, most of the details have to be worked out with the doctor. The birth plan will provide all medical information and L&D strategies agreed upon by your partner and the doctor. To help you get involved with the plan, your task will be to take all the information and organize it into one concise document to be used on D-Day. I will only provide you general direction of what the document should contain because I want you to create your own plan so that you will have a thorough understanding.

Goal Statement

If you are going to try limited intervention and do not want to have an epidural, at the very top of the plan in bold letters state

"I want a Natural Birth with NO Medical intervention. Do not ask me if I want any form of pain medication at any time!"

You could also add statements like:

"We are a team! Let's do this together!

"I CAN NOT accomplish my goal without your help and encouragement"

These statements will speak directly to the nurses and other medical staff of your goal and will hopefully get them on board.

Baby Gender

Identify the baby's gender if it is known. If you and your partner are waiting until the doctor announces it in the L&D room, then you should also in bold state:

"GENDER UNKNOWN. It will be a surprise to us all."

To help with any confusion, you could assign a gender upfront and make sure the staff is constantly referring to "her" or "him" when doing the regular checkups. This is a tough one, so try not to think about it too much if the gender is going to be a surprise. I think our nurses were playing games with me by referring on one visit as "he" and then on the next as "her", confusing but it was better than referring to the baby as "it".

Active Labor

In this section of the plan your partner and your doctor need to work out the details of what she wants to do if certain health issues arise with the Labor and Delivery. Here are some questions to consider:

1.   What can we do to speed up the contractions naturally so that your partner can move into transition labor more quickly? There are multiple options like scrapping the cervix or breaking the bag of waters.

2.   What conditions must exist for the doctor to recommend

medical intervention with Pitocin? If the bag has broken, and it has been a few hours and contractions are not progressing there is a risk of infection. To reduce exposure time Pitocin might be recommended.

3. What are the pain medications available and what are the potential issues? What are the restrictions placed on the mother once pain treatment is given? If you get on an opioid you might be limited to the bed or to movement near the bed only.

4. How long does it take to get an epidural to be administered? What are the restrictions placed on the mother once the epidural is given? Once the epidural is given, she will be locked down to the bed. There is no walking. Mostly because she is not physically able to walk!

5. What conditions must exist for a C-section to be recommended? See doctor's recommendation.

Once your partner and doctor have worked out all the details you can formulate a plan. You should use the conditions set by the doctor as decision points and act accordingly. In my opinion your plan should start out with the goal to go unmedicated with no interventions and have interventions planned for at certain decision points. Obviously, your plan should be flexible and should have a decision point to relinquish all control over to the doctor once the mother or baby are having a problem.

Transition Labor

Once in transition labor, the mother and baby are at the most risk and where the doctor's experience is required for a successful birth. There are tools available to the doctor that might be used if the situation requires their implementation. These tools pose certain physical risk to the baby and the mother and should be considered with the doctor:

1. Lubrication -petroleum jelly used to reduce friction around the pelvic bone. Doctor will need to verify if your partner is allergic to the product.
2. Vacuum suction- a suction cup device applied to the head of the baby provides a grip to pull the baby out of the canal. As you might imagine there are possible spinal and head injuries associated with this method.
3. Forceps - a tong like device that is used to grab the baby under the jaw and ear to help pull the baby out of the canal. Like suction devices there is a risk of spinal and head injuries.

Post Delivery

When your partner goes into transition labor and starts pushing, the room will fill up with nurses. Each have their specific tasks for the delivery and others have tasks once the baby is in the world. Your birth plan offers a means to slow the process down once the baby is here so that your goals are achieved. Below are some post-delivery topics you and your partner need to discuss up front and put in the Birth Plan:

Skin to Skin – your plan should instruct the doctor or nurse to place the baby on the mother's chest immediately after birth. Do not wait for a bath or to towel off the baby. The baby will still be connected to the umbilical cord. Do not delay this moment. If for some reason mom is not capable of holding the baby, then you should hold the baby on her chest. The last resort, you take your shirt off and hold the baby. This act is all about the release of oxytocin and bonding.

Cord blood – Cord blood can be banked and utilized at later date for hematopoietic and genetic disorders. The stem cells in the chord can be used to treat the disease. If you want to bank the blood there are services available, but the doctor must know up front because there is a short window, like 30 seconds, before the cord is drained. Unfortunately, banking cord blood cost money. Your doctor will be able to provide you the information. If you choose not to bank the cord blood, then you will need to decide if you want the cord to pulsate for a few minutes before cutting.

There is no right or wrong here, to me it just makes since for the final transfer of nutrients from the mother to the baby be completed. Because I am cheap and don't want to pay for cord blood banking, my vote is to let the cord drain dry.

Baby's Location – there will be lots of activities going on in the room once the baby is born. Nurses will be in queue with their tasks to get your bundle ready for the world. Your plan should specifically state the baby is to not leave the room unless accompanied by someone identified on your Birth Plan. If kidnapping was the first reason that came to your mind when I suggested keeping your baby in the room, then you watch way too much CSI. In reality, a CSI baby theft is rarer than getting hit by lightning. The actual reason for keeping the baby in the room is to keep Mom from freaking out. Mothers who just meet their baby for the first time are filled full of hormones that are affecting the chemistry of their brain. If the baby is not in her arms or if she cannot see the baby, there is a real chance of her having a panic attack. In the event the baby does have to leave the room, she will be comforted that a loved one is still caring for the baby. Most likely the Mom will be on bed rest for a few hours after the delivery so you will have to reassure her of the baby's safety.

Eye Salve – Also known as antibiotic ointment or erythromycin. When the baby is born their eyes are very vulnerable to infections, especially when going through the birth canal. If the mother has gonorrhea or chlamydia, the easiest place for the bacteria to be transmitted is in the baby's eyes. Most states require the eye salve to be applied at birth thus providing some protection So check with your doctor if you want to abstain from the practice. If it is required or needed, it can be applied after the mother has had some skin to skin time. Ask your doctor about how long you can wait before issues arise, but it is not necessary for the nurse to take the baby before mom is ready.

Vaccinations – once the baby is in the world it no longer has its mother's immune system to protect it. The American Academy of Pediatrics (AAP) and the Center of Disease Control (CDC) recommend the following vaccinations be given on day 1. It is not necessary they are given immediately after birth and can wait a few hours.

1. Vitamin K treatment – babies are deficient in Vitamin K at birth and need it to be supplemented to help with blood clotting.

2. HepB Vaccination – Hepatitis B is a virus that is transmitted through body fluids and blood. It causes chronic liver and kidney disease.

I know there is a lot of cultural taboo and uncertainty out there about vaccinations. Here is my opinion and the opinion of every Pediatric Doctor who is not a conspiracy theorist: Vaccines are good and should be given to every child at the recommended interval. Here is a fact: there is no credible evidence that concludes your child will have autism from a vaccine. Go to www.cdc.gov/vaccines

for more information. If you can find the scientific evidence that shows correlation and causation that vaccines cause autism, please notify the CDC so they can begin burning down their entire organization.

The Birth Plan contains lots of information and can be a little cumbersome. But when you organize all the information, choices, and outcomes into one location you will feel like you have more control over the situation. With that feeling of control, a little more peace of mind will settle in over the pregnancy. The birth plan will give you the razor-sharp ability to react rationally to whatever L&D throws at you. In the last few chapters I walk through the L&D of all three of my girls where I demonstrate how we used our birth plan.

Chapter 5.5:
Yoga Balls, Contraction Meditation and Visualization

We have all seen an L&D movie that has a plot with jokes that are more preferred by our partner than us. You know the movie where the guy and the pregnant girl are sitting in some studio practicing that famous Lamaze breathing: eeh whooo, eeh whooo, eeh whooo. For this one scene I have to say Hollywood got it right as far as what the class offers. There are real classes out there that do teach L&D breathing. In the Lamaze class I took, I practiced the rhythm breathing with my wife. Ironically, based on my experience with the delivery of three girls, I am not sure the breathing rhythm works. It especially doesn't work when the baby is pushing against the mother's pelvic bone and her body just wants to grunt and yell. There is no rhythm breathing, just her trying to catch her breath.

So, would I recommend that you take a Lamaze class with her? Yes, of course. It doesn't hurt to get into the moment with her and learn more about the labor and delivery. The problem I found on our search for a good Lamaze class was that it was like finding a good kick boxing class— some kick boxing class makes you think you can walk into a ring with Jean Claud Van Dam and others make you think punching and kicking are dance moves that should occur simultaneously. If the area you are in does not offer an in-depth Lamaze class for coping with L&D, I would still take the class. The class is more about the two of you getting connected to the pregnancy. Hey, another good Daddy Doula Date Night!

If the class you attend is not as fulfilling as you would like, below are some concepts that you both can practice. The Lamaze class I attended introduced using Yoga Balls as a tool and a relaxation technique to promote the labor. I combined the information I learned in the class with some other life experiences that not only helped my wife and I connect, but worked for her during the L&D.

1.   Yoga Balls

2.   Contraction Meditation

3.   L&D Visualization

Yoga Ball.

I am sure you have seen those big colored plastic inflatable balls on infomercials and rolling around the gym. The balls are used by yogis and others trying to get a little more flexible. The ball can also be used as a workout tool. For your pregnant wife it can help get the baby into position or to take the edge off a contraction. The Lamaze class that I took focused heavily on using the ball as a tool to help with positioning the baby and helping the mother take pressure off her back. Here are a couple of positions your partner can use during Pre and Active Labor:

1.   Sitting on the Ball: Have your partner sit on the ball with a wide stance to give her balance. She should be able to

bounce and swirl her hips without falling over. The ball allows gravity to help the baby get further down into the canal. When she is setting on the ball all you must do is make sure she does not fall off.

2. Using the Ball as a Bench: For this position she would get on her knees and lie across the ball to rests her head. This will help relieve back pressure. This stance positions her stomach bulging down and can help rotate the baby if the baby is facing upwards by using the baby's natural center of gravity. Facing down is the preferred position of the baby when in transition. If the baby comes out chin up (aka sunny side up), it is more difficult to get the head past the pelvic bone because the neck cannot bend back as far as it can forward. And the more difficulty the baby has moving out the birth canal, the more pain your partner is going to experience.

The ball is a great tool to have around the house. It is a good platform to practice your massage techniques and to spoil her with attention. It is also a great L&D tool. In Chapter 8 Hands of Silk and Stone I will provide some great massage techniques. In the last few weeks of the pregnancy, my wife was constantly bouncing. By the end of the 36 weeks gestation, Momma was ready to move that baby down into the canal. When we got to the delivery room, we rotated between sitting, benching, and standing as a part of our L&D coping exercises. It also offered me a seat when she was leaning against the bed. Make sure you ask the hospital if they offer one in the L&D room because it will be one last thing to pack. Those balls take some energy to blow up with a hand pump!

Contraction Meditation

As stated previously the Lamaze class we attended was like the movie stereo type. Over the years I have learned that keeping an open mind when in situations that are annoying or boring, you can actually find a few golden nuggets. One of those golden nuggets from this Lamaze class was that to make the delivery quicker, we must get our partner to relax as much as possible, both during and after a contraction. It is almost non-intuitive, but the more relaxed the mother is during the contraction the more the uterus will open when it is flexing. The more the uterus opens on each contraction the shorter the labor time. In the Lamaze class we learned a relaxation technique that required us to lie on the ground while I massaged and tickled my wife as she focused on soft breathing. My job was to talk to her by telling her a sweet story from our past and guide her to relaxation. At first my wife and I practiced the exercise just like we were taught in the class. But I found that she never really relaxed even though she was not being stressed by a real contraction. I also noticed the exercise seemed to focus more on me talking and her breathing. Before we move further let me remind you of what a contraction is so you can understand what we are trying to accomplish.

During a contraction, the mother is experiencing her uterus flexing with enormous power. Her body is preparing to squeeze a four-inch diameter head out of a one-inch opening. The closest I can put it in guy terms is imagine you are squatting your body weight when suddenly both your quads start cramping and you have no choice but to get upright before the pain ends. You succeed but only get a one-minute break and you must do it again, and again, and again for hours.

With that pain in mind, I knew something was missing in the exercise. I need a tool or something that could actually get her to relax. After some reflection, I discovered that the only way I personally knew how to accomplish real relaxation in my life was through meditation. I figured if I applied the Lamaze class story while implementing meditation techniques during a contraction, my wife might have a chance to achieve some form of calm. Over many years, I have been experimenting with concepts of Meditation and found that focused breathing (counting your breaths) was a good means for me to relax and shed day to day stress. One night during our relaxation sessions, I decided to walk my wife through a relaxation technique called progressive meditation. I usually practice this technique right before bed and it usually lasts about 10 minutes. The first 5 minutes are for getting my body relaxed and the other 5 minutes are for me to calm my mind. The problem I had to solve for my wife was how to compress the time it takes to relax into the time of a contraction and how to do it with every contraction. With a few tweaks of the ancient technique I came up with a version I call Contraction Meditation. For this type of meditation, you will guide your partner through the little mini-meditation sessions to promote her overall all relaxation during labor contraction versus fighting against her body every contraction. If she can get her body completely relaxed during active labor, when the uterus is contracting like a Rhonda Rouse arm-bar submission, then she could be a secret Shaolin Monk. If the two of you are like my wife and I, Contraction Meditations will become impossible for the latter stages of active labor. However, for pre-labor and early into active labor, the contraction meditations helped with her overall anxiety and kept her generally relaxed. In one session, she actually fell asleep because the contraction interval became so spread out. I encourage you to seek out meditation classes or apps like www.headspace.com to help you practice meditation. At a minimum, you will get a better feel for the breathing and could find some self-awareness along the way. But if meditation for the sake of self-awareness seems a little too weird, below are the concepts that you can use to practice Contraction Meditation that will help you connect with your partner and help her relax during pre-labor.

Contraction Meditation Practice

To practice contraction mediation, you have to find a way to simulate a contraction. Unless you can get your partner to experience leg cramps on-demand, then you can try the old ice bag trick to make her uncomfortable and agitated. What is the old ice bag trick? It is not quite the Ice Bucket Challenge, but it can have a chilling effect. Basically, you are going to insert a 1- gallon zip lock bag of ice up your partner's shirt in the middle of meditation. Even if she is mentally prepared for it, the ice will still cause her to squirm and tense up. You will also need a stopwatch to simulate the contraction duration and the rest period.

To get started you need to make your partner as comfortable as possible lying on the floor, in the bed, or using the yoga ball. If you are not as comfortable as her, go with it because it is part of the Daddy Doula deal you signed up for because you will not be comfortable in the hospital. Spoon her, massage her, and tickle her back. It does not matter what you are doing as long as she is enjoying your warmth and love. As the Daddy Doula, you are her guide in the meditation. Your voice is going to set her breathing rhythms and walk her through her mental journey. So be gentle, soft, and smooth like James Earl Jones.

There are three phases to the contraction meditation that you must learn to be her guide:

1. Mental Journey to somewhere personal and relaxing

2. Meditation technique called progressive relaxation

3. Simulate the contraction

Phase 1 is designed to set up the environment in her mind for relaxation. A good way to create a sense of relaxation in her mind is to send her mind's eye somewhere that elicits comfort. You might know of a place that would provide the desired effect, but as part of the connection activity you should get her to create the place for you. This thought experiment might not be natural to her, or to you, so asking the right questions can help stimulate her imagination. The key to the questions is specificity. The more information and descriptions you have, the closer she can come to reliving the experience. Below are some questions that you can ask her to get you started. You will get the general understanding of the nature of the questions and will be able to ask your own to get the required details. I also suggest that you write down the information you receive so you can always take her back to the same moment for each relaxation session.

1.   Where is the location that you would like to visit with me? Somewhere you felt comfortable and safe.

2.   What is the place's temperature?

3.   What does the sky look like?

4.   What does the landscape look like?

5.   Are there any smells in the air?

6.   What sounds do you hear?

7.   How do you feel? Loved? Happy? Safe? Why?

Phase 1 should be used at the beginning of each relaxation session or during L&D. It should last between 2 and 3 minutes. Once you are into the contraction phase, there will be no need to keep going back to the story. The intent of phase 1 is to set the mood only and the story can begin as soon as she is situated comfortably. As meditation becomes more natural and it becomes easier to get into a relaxing mind set, Phase 1 can be skipped. But because you are also trying to connect on an emotional level, having her mind continually revisit one of the best moments in the relationship can only promote your overall Daddy Doula status.

Phase 2 is the key to Contraction Meditation. The progressive relaxation technique will help your partner enter a state of deep relaxation. For the practice sessions, I want you to go through the entire progression before you start the contraction simulation. By completing the progression each practice session, not only will you get really good at being a guide, your partner will have multiple opportunities to experience real relaxation. Early on in Pre-Labor you can probably cycle through the progression for each contraction, but the closer she gets to the 2:1:1 ratio the harder it is for her to have any time to relax and you will have to use Phase 3 techniques. The phase 2 basic formula for progressive relaxation is as follows:

1. Deeply inhale through the nose and exhale from the mouth 4 times. The breaths should be so deep that you can hear them from a few feet.

2. On the last exhale, instruct her to let her breaths return to normal and focus on the rising and falling of her chest as the air enters and leaves her lungs.

3. After about 30 seconds of normal breathing ask her to take a deep breath and flex her feet and calves real hard for about 3 seconds. This works best if you instruct her to start the flex on the inhale and release the flex on the

exhale. Instruct her to let her breathing return to normal.

4. Over the next 30 seconds you can massage the feet and calves very gently. Once complete, vocalize to her in your soft gentle voice that her feet and calves are now completely relaxed. (See Hands of Silk and Stone Chapter for massaging techniques.)

5. Move to the next section of her body and repeat 2 through 4.

    - thighs and butt

    - lower back,

    - upper back and shoulders, arms,

    - hands and fingers

Do not worry if you finish up quicker than 10 minutes. Fill the time with light touching to keep the energy between the two of you flowing.

Phase 3 is where you will make your impact as a Daddy Doula. The Daddy Doula rule here is any relaxation is better than none. You will have to use the progression technique but speed up the process because of the length of contractions. In this phase, you will only focus on her relaxing the area under stress. For the simulation, your stress area will be where you place the ice bag. I want you to place the ice bag on her body for 3 minutes then remove it for a 2-minute break. Repeat until the ice is melted or 30 minutes has expired. If you really want to keep the ice challenge at its maximum difficulty, you could prepare a cooler of ice bags to exchange out when the ice starts to melt. Fresh bags may seem a little cruel, but it will get maximum affect. Be careful to monitor the skin under the ice bag for ice burn.

This is the basic Phase 3 simulation formula:

1. Right after you have completed Phase 2 make sure your partner is on her stomach or side. Slide the ice bag under her shirt and start the timer. You can use an ace wrap to secure it in place so that it does not slide off.

2. Ask her to take 4 deep exaggerated breaths as described in Phase 2.

3. Most likely her breathing will not return to normal but ask her to identify the muscles that are tensed up. She does not have to vocalize them to you; just acknowledge them in her mind.

4. You quickly observe her body and try to identify the tense muscles. If you placed the ice on her lower back, most likely the area tensing up will be her back, shoulders and legs because they are closest to the ice.

5. Pick one muscle group above the ice and start the progression technique. Ask her to flex it for 3 seconds and then release. Same breathing method as in Phase 2. Massage the relaxed area for 30 seconds and move to the

next muscle group.

6.   Pick one muscle group below the ice and start the progression technique. Ask her to flex it for 3 seconds and then release. Same breathing method as in Phase 2. Massage the relaxed area for 30 seconds and move to the next muscle group.

7.   On the third progression, choose the area with the ice. In this case, we have assumed the lower back. Ask her to flex it for 3 seconds and relax. The relaxation period should go until the 3-minute ice session is over. No massaging required, but you can apply gentle touches to other areas until the 3 minutes expires.

8.   Remove the ice. Continue to massage and talk to her until the two-minute break is over. See Chapter 5: Words of Affirmation for details.

9.   Add ice bag for round 2. Do not apply to the same area. Most likely it has started to go numb because the nerve endings are frozen. Back and legs are always good locations to get maximum freezing affect.

For D-Day, the only difference in the contraction meditation, other than the ice, is the interval between contractions. On D-day the stress area will be her uterus. If you are wondering how your partner is going to flex her uterus, then I ask you to remember the squatting analogy and know that her body will be doing all the flexing for her. In Phase 3 the contraction rhythm is going to set your pace. If the contractions are 5 minutes apart, then you have 5 minutes to get her relaxed before the next contraction starts. If they are 1-minute apart Daddy Doula is going to be working hard. In Pre-Labor, contractions can very between 5 and 30 minutes apart. In Active Labor, it can vary between 5 minutes and 30 seconds apart. I do not want to prescribe a formula for real contractions because your partner will be going through something extraordinary where using instincts tend to play out better than predetermined methods. Just apply the progression techniques you have learned, and like the great champions, practice will fine-tune your ability and trained instincts will guide you to victory.

L&D Visualization

L&D Visualization is like meditation, but it is not meant to be relaxing. It is intended to stimulate and prepare you. The practice of visualization is common among professional athletes. The athlete will visualize certain scenarios of the game where the pressure is on and he has to come through with the game winning shot, set the perfect block, or make a slim read over the linebacker for the TD.

So why do athletes visualize moments in the game? Not only does it focus them on the game plan and their role, but it also alleviates the anxiety of the moment. When their number is called to take the game on, they have already been there, did it, and succeeded. So why not do the same for the delivery of your baby?

The easiest way to start visualizing the birth is to start with the Birth Plan. Your partner has her role and you have yours. For the visualization exercise, ensure you both run through the process at the same time. I would recommend sitting on the couch together holding hands and listening to some easy-going music you both like.

To start the visualization, identify the scenario in the Birth Plan you are going to be playing out. Get comfortable, close your eyes, and begin to take the journey in your mind's eye. Sit silently playing out the scenario and using the birth plan in your own thoughts. I would suggest you set a timer and allow the visualization to take a total of 10 to 12 minutes. You could break the visualization up into the three phases of labor and use an alarm to signify the start of the next phase. This will make it easier to implement your birth plan. During the first practice assume the best-case scenario where you are both at home, it is Saturday morning, and the contractions begin. Go through pre-labor, driving to the hospital, checking in, getting into the L&D room, labor progressing, then the baby arriving. Get detailed in your mind's eye. See yourself behind the wheel taking the turns at each stop sign. Mostly see yourself in the L&D room being Daddy Doula, and then you are encouraging your partner pushing until the head magically crowns. See yourself cutting the umbilical cord. Feel the success of the moment when you hear that sweet happy cry. Feel the warmth of the baby's hand as it grasps your finger for the first time and turns your Clint Eastwood heart into a gushy pile of man goo. When the final alarm sounds, give yourself a minute to account for your feelings then go over some of the details your mind encountered during the visualization with your partner. This will help the two of you get on the same page and connect to the moment. It will also allow the two of you to set reasonable expectations of how each of you will use the birth plan.

The next time you visualize the L&D, change the scenario up by throwing in some challenges and see how you react to the situation when you apply your birth plan. I'll give you a few challenges to consider, but it will be up to you how you include them into your birth plan and how to walk them in your minds journey. WARNING! The post L&D visualization wrap-up with your partner regarding some of these challenges might be emotional and hard to handle. My suggestion is talk them out and try to accept the person's emotions no matter how irrational it might seem.

Pre-Labor

- You are at work when you get the call to come home.

- You are stuck in rush hour traffic and contractions are 5 minutes apart.

- Her water breaks at home and you are an hour away.

- Labor begins and she is at the mall on the other side of town and you are at home.

- It is snowing/raining and contractions are 10 minutes apart and you are at your grandparent's house.

Active Labor

- It has been snowing/raining for 8 hours and the contractions are now 3 minutes apart and you are at your grandparent's house.

- While at the hospital, the nurse reports the Baby's heart rate keeps dropping during contractions but recovers after a few minutes. Nurses are informing you of the problem.

- Nurse comes into the room to offer Pitocin without offering to try other natural methods to get the labor progressing.

- The Nurse breaks the bag-of-water or strips the membrane to thin it, but hours later nothing is working to progress contractions. Baby's heart rate is healthy. When will you concede for additional medical intervention?

- The pain of the contractions seems to be crippling your partner. Nurses ask you if you want the epidural started.

Transition - Delivery

- Baby comes into the world and you hear the first cry of life.

- Baby is sunny side up and pressing on the pelvic bone. (See doctor's notes for information)

- Umbilical cord is wrapped around baby's throat. (See doctor's notes for information)

- Complications that lead to a C-Section. (See doctor's notes for information)

- Your partner perineum tears, and she starts to bleed. (See doctor's notes for information)

- Extra Bleeding of the uterus after birth. (See doctor's notes for information)

For the most part transition labor is where all the medical crazy happens. My list included scenarios that will be difficult even if you imagine them. I put the "see doctor's notes for information" so that you can get exact information from your doctor regarding these situations. They can be added to your birth plan so you can have a handy reminder of what is going to happen in each circumstance. Visualizing these tough scenarios will help you emotionally if you start to ponder how you will react if the crazy does happen. Be comforted by the fact that no matter how extreme the situation, the doctor will react based on training and experience. The actions taken will most likely be the right move for both the baby and mother. To ensure that you do not pass out when you see a gush of blood or when you don't hear your baby cry within minutes of being dropped into the world, know how your doctor will respond is essential to your emotional balance.

Remember in the US most deliveries are successful, and the mother and baby have really low mortality rates because most issues are detected early and can be mitigated by C-sections. Most deaths in delivery room are like car accidents, unexpected and out of the control of the unexpected driver who was hit by a random raging vehicle.

Practicing with the Yoga Balls and using Contraction Meditation with L&D visualization are essential to your partner connecting to you. I highly recommend you practice all three methods laid out above at least twice per week for 30 minutes. Trust me on this, if you are constantly initiating the practice your partner will recognize your effort and the trust in you as her daddy Doula will be solidified. There will be no doubt of your training on D-Day when you are calm and relaxed when the craziness of L&D decides to veer you off your original plan.

Chapter 5.6:
First Aid and CPR Class

I am very fortunate that my job provides annual First Aid and CPR training. It is easy to keep in the loop about the latest strategies being used by personnel in your local police, fire, and EMT departments. Over the last decade the chest to breath ratio has changed, as well the strategies for drowning and heart attacks. If your job does not offer CPR and First Aid certification, contact your local Fire Department, Red Cross, or Hospital and find out when they are providing courses. The course is usually around 5 hours.

I do not want to go into the subject matter of the class because it would be irresponsible of me to provide you any type of CPR training. But what I will tell you is this, if you do one thing before your baby is born take a CPR and First Aid class. Not only does it give you some basic training on what to do, the class also will help you deal with the initial stress of an emergency. Most of us will never deal with a severe first aid or a life threating situation, so we truly never will know how we would react. But I believe that the more knowledge you have about an emergency situation, the calmer, more confident, and more rational you become in the moment.

Can you imagine your emotional state the second after you realize your kid is choking on a gold fish cracker, or has fallen on his head and is not crying, or when he flips over in the bath tub face down when you were reaching for the soap? I would imagine like most unprepared parents, pure panic. But I believe with some training and knowledge that panic only lasts for one second and the next second you have assessed the situation of the threats and began acting swiftly and accurately. I believe you should take CPR and first aid classes at least annually so that you will be prepared for any small medical emergency. Imagine if you were CPR and First Aid trained and there is a zombie apocalypse. You could be the only person in your group who can keep someone alive. In the post-apocalyptic world, you will be known as "Doc"!

There is one topic in most CPR and first aid classes that always seems to get touched on, but never really explained well. That topic is the AED, Automated Electronic Defibrillator. In the 21st Century, I would be surprised if a building or office did not have an AED. The device is literally a life saver and can easily be operated by anyone. The problem is the general public is not trained on how to use them and has been misled by medical sitcoms and movies on what the technology actually does to save the life of the person in need. I also think that instructors take for granted the intuitive nature of the newer devices and feel that they do not really need explain the device in detail in the classes.

So, what is an AED? You have probably seen a yellow or red box hanging on a wall at your local arena, municipal building, or big box store that has a sign above it that reads "AED. Call 911". In that little box is a computer, a battery, and wires with little pads. To operate the AED, generally all you do is open the box and attach the pads to the person who is dying of a heart attack or has drowned. If you were like me, before I had my CPR training, I thought that little box was going to deliver some amazing voltage to the dead guy with enough force to make his back arch up. The shock would make the dead guy start shaking until suddenly he surprisingly becomes alert. Unfortunately, the movies have misled us again. "The Cart" in an emergency room is not the same as an AED. An AED will not bring a non-beating heart back to life. The only thing an AED will do is reset the heartbeat rhythm of a fluttering heart (fibrillation). Here is an anecdote that will help explain the how not to use an AED.

Two 50-year-old guys are working out hard in the cross-training area of the gym. They are doing their best imitation of Beach Body's Insanity®. They both suddenly feel lightheaded and hit the floor. A few minutes pass and a couple of other patrons notice that the two guys are down and not moving. Our uncertified heroes rush over to assess the situation. Breathing and pulses are checked on both fallen men, and nothing is detected. The heroes yell for the AEDs and to call 911. This gym has First Generation AEDs that do not meet current standards but provides the appropriate shock if needed. Hero 1 hooks up the AED to his down comrade per the written instructions. Hero 2 hooks up his First-Generation AED to his fallen comrade per the written instructions. Both AEDs go through the computerized routine and one begins to flash. There is nothing more the heroes can do except wait for the EMTs. Right?

After a few minutes Hero 1 notices his AED machine is not doing the same thing as Hero 2's AED. Hero 2's AED is advising that a shock is about to be administered. Hero 1s machine is reporting nothing. Hero 1 thinks the machine is busted and calls for another AED. Hero 1 hooks up the replacement AED per the instructions. He sits back and waits. Nothing. The AED is still not advising of the shock. 10 minutes have passed and finally the EMTs show up. Hero 2 reports his AED has been providing shocks every few minutes. Hero 1 is pissed because his AED has done nothing. He strongly informs the EMT that he has hooked up the AED to his comrade and the machine will not shock him back to life like the other AED is doing to Hero 2s comrade. The EMT shook his head in disbelief and asked if chest compression and breaths had been given while he was in route. Hero 1 and 2 were shaken, because neither performed any CPR. They thought the purpose of the AED was to jolt life back into their comrades. The EMTs checked both men. Hero 1's man has been dead for 10 minutes. Hero's 2s man is barely hanging on. The EMTs rush Hero 2's man out to get him to the Emergency room as fast as possible. So, what was the difference in the two men's situation and how the AED performed.

Comrade 1 had a massive heart attack and his heart was no longer beating when the AED was hooked up. The AED diagnosed the situation and waited for the heart to begin beating again. This is where CPR helps the AED work.

Comrade 2 had a massive heart attack and his heart was fluttering like a fish out of water. The AED diagnosed the erratic heartbeat and applied an electric jolt to the heart. The jolt normalized the heartbeat momentarily. Every time it began to flutter another jolt was applied. The heart never stopped beating.

To sum up quickly on what happened with our heroes and fallen comrades. Both Heroes applied the AEDs correctly. Both AEDs, and the backup, worked like each was designed. Hero 1 and 2 should have been administering chest compressions and breaths until either became responsive, or the EMT arrived. The good news about this anecdote is most new AEDs have instructions that include the compression intervals and breaths so this situation would most likely not happen. Some even have a metronome to set the appropriate pace of compressions. But in either case, if the Heroes would have been CPR trained, they would have administered chest compressions once the fallen comrades were deemed unresponsive.

CPR and First Aid training is an essential part of being prepared for bringing a new life into the world. It is an opportunity for you and the mother to learn about the not so comfortable parts of life and how to handle emergencies in a calm and productive manner. Parents do what they can to protect their kids from harm by padding the corners, plugging the sockets, and locking the cabinets. Like it or not, the craziest most unexpected accidents will happen. Bumps, bruises, and a little blood will be seen at some point. The question is will you be the parent that is screaming and running around like Jar Jar Binx when your child trips and falls through the glass coffee table, or cool like George Clooney ready to assist your child in the emergency. The added bonus to taking the CPR and First Aid class with the mother, is that you get some real "Doula" credit and will have another experience to grow that needed connection.

Chapter 5.7:

Create a Fire escape plan

A fire escape plan might seem like a bit of over kill when it comes to home safety, but you are looking for activities that you can do with the expecting mother that will grow the two of you closer emotionally. And what says emotional connection better than the feeling of safety?

The basics of a home fire escape plan, and an associated map, are as follows:

1. Determine your muster point and put a big red cross on your map. Even if you are evacuating from the same room, you still need to identify this location in the event you get separated during the evacuation. The muster point should be outside of the house and far enough away that the fire truck will not run you over when it comes screaming down the road.

2. Identify the locations of all fire extinguishers, fire blankets, and other safety equipment. It would be best if the equipment was in one location together. If you have not purchased the equipment previously, here is another event you and the expecting mom can do together. There are a few retail companies out there that you can buy all the safety equipment. Just make a day out of it and have

fun. This is a shopping event you can take the lead and has nothing to do with colors or cuteness.

3.   Identify all points of exit from every room. An exit should not be breaking a wall or window to get out. Save that for the last case scenario! If you have an upstairs, roll up ladders secured to the wall at the windows can be used for top floor escapes. If the stairs are your only option, then make sure a fire blanket is accessible. A fire blanket can be used to protect you from indirect flames just long enough for someone to run down a few flights of stairs. Refer to your list of safety equipment that will assist in your routes and make sure there is enough equipment for each person in the house.

4.   Identify where everybody sleeps on the map, including the pets.

5.   All exits should show a route to the muster point.

Please be aware that some sleeping children do not respond to smoke alarms. Your plan should not expect children to awaken and evacuate. Have your escape plan assign someone to get a child.

Here is a general idea of what your map should look like.

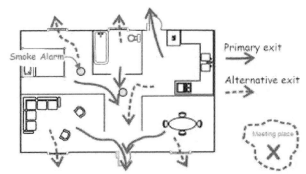

Now that you have a plan, you must practice. I suggest the days you change the batteries on your smoke detector, you also run your fire drill. It can become a little family event that everyone begrudgingly does but knows it gets rewarded with ice-cream and pizza, or whatever is the family junk food of choice.

Chapter 6:
Commitment to Health

One of the most amazing feelings about bringing a child into the world is the sentiment that you can correct some of the wrongs of your life and make the next generation of your bloodline stronger, smarter, and more loving than the previous generation. Usually if that feeling comes to your heart, then so will the following realization that you will have to change some of your bad habits to ensure your child will grow to his or her full potential. The good news is that you and your partner have 7 to 9 months to change your life in the direction you want that will ensure your baby comes into the world with a healthy mother and father. The last connection activity is Commitment to Health. Of all the things that you can do to improve yourself in the next few months, health should be your priority. In my opinion, a person who is in good health is more confident, dedicated to life, and generally a happier person in the world. Does a healthier person have these three traits because they physically look better to their peers? Maybe. But I believe a healthy person takes on these traits because they become aware of themselves and understand what it takes to make sacrifices every day. For instance, it is hard to turn away from all the fast food joints on every corner instead of cooking a good meal when you have already been at work for 12 hours. The world we live in is fast, congested, and surrounded by a 1000 quick fixes. I am not going to suggest another quick fix. The concepts in the section could literally change you and your partner's life forever if each of you extends the healthy mind set beyond the pregnancy time period. I am proposing a lifelong commitment where the next 6 to 9 months can be used as springboard for the two of you to become the healthy parents you each want to be.

Generally, I am going to focus on you because I want you to be the best Daddy Doula, but your partner has to be on the health train for you to be successful. If she is not, you might find that you are reconfiguring your stomach to match the roundness and plumpness of your partner's childbearing mid-section. But I know you are different because you are reading this book. You are going to be a Daddy Doula and you can become the catalyst for both you and your partner to start leading a healthy lifestyle. And based on what you have learned thus far about L&D, you know that to do all the walking, massaging, and home improvements this book is suggesting, if you don't start exercising, you are going to be one tired and sore daddy after miles of pre labor laps, hundreds of squats, and hours of massaging.

If I was a betting man, I would wager that in the last 10 years you have read an article about a miracle diet and you tried that diet for a few weeks, or longer, but ultimately failed. Most likely Vegas would be paying out that bet because I know I certainly have tried and failed. Here is the gist of my story. I used to be like a lot of men in modern America who after college found themselves overweight and not anywhere close to my youthful leanness. Between the age of 20 and 30 I went from the athletic star goalkeeper on the High school pitch to an overweight PlayStation FIFA champion on my couch. I also really loved my beer and late-night fast food restaurants. At 30 I decided to have a general physical where the doctor checked my blood glucose, triglycerides, vitamins, STDs, etc. A full blood panel for everything health related. The results were crazy! The good news was that I had nothing that could kill me in the short term. On the other hand, death at 50 was a great possibility with my cholesterol, triglycerides, and glucose levels so far above the acceptable level that my doctor said if this blood work panel was from an out of shape 50-year-old, she would be recommending heart disease prescriptions to help reduce risks of stroke or heart attack. During my visit the Doc gave me the angry coach's half time speech I needed while reminding me that both my parents had major heart attacks at 50. When I left her office that day, I knew I needed to do something different if I wanted to be a healthy old man. Fortunately, I already knew how to work-out because of my competitive sports background. What I really did not know how to do was eat. I grew up in South Georgia where everything was cooked with butter and covered in gravy (white, red, or brown). I ate vegetables as long as they were covered in cheese and loved a good salad with lots of ranch dressing. In short, my idea of healthy food was skewed. Thankfully I meet my soon to be wife a few months after receiving that dreadful health report, because she was more familiar with healthier eating. Overtime she was the one who really pushed me to start eating the right way on a regular basis. She is not much of a fast food girl and enjoys simple cooking so dinners with her rarely included a bucket and plastic sporks. With the combination of my exercising and her teaching me new eating habits, I have finally recovered. I am at a healthy 18% body fat, my cholesterol and triglycerides are in check, and there are no signs of diabetes or heart disease.

My time and experiences recreating the healthier me I developed this philosophy:

A healthy man is a healthy father. A healthy father is a man who will bestow amazing love and wisdom to his kids not only through words, but through his example.

If you find that you are more in line with the belief that you are "Not in Good Shape", don't' worry because you are still a young machine capable of so much more than you might think. Because you are young, your body can bounce back rather quickly if you give it the right motivation and fuel. (I am assuming you are under the age of 50 if you are reading this book. If you are over 50 and having a baby, you are the man!).

Here is something to ponder as you read this section. A University College of London study has shown that if an activity is committed to for 66 days, then the activity will become a habit. In my journey I found that after about 30 days of eating well and exercising regularly I had created a new trend in my life. After about 60 days, I found that it was truly a weekly habit for me to exercise and eat well. After about 90 days I knew that I changed my lifestyle and was conscious of the fact that I did not exercise that week or eat the way I had been the previous week. For me, even after slacking for a week, because of the gains I saw, it was not hard for me to get back to my new normal. So how did I get my health back? I created the habit of 80/20 eating and applying the Slow Start Rule to exercising.

Chapter 6.1:
80/20 Eating

When it comes to being healthy, the first thing that is advertised is you must lose all that unwanted weight. And we are told the quickest way to lose this unwanted weight is through our diet. Well they are correct about the diet being the key to losing the weight part. The problem is most are advertising the "quick fix meal plan" and not the "long term maintains the good weight plan". I have tried many of the quick fix methods advertised: low carb diets, no carb diets, and counting calories. But like many who tried I have always failed when attempting these fad diets. I would start off on fire and lose 10 pounds. Then on my first challenge of will power I would crash right into the All- You-Can-Eat Buffet.

At first, I thought it was me. I believed that I did not have the discipline or desire to complete the programs. When I reflect back on those times, discipline was probably 25% of the reason, the remainder was motivation. The biggest reason I failed was because I had to stop enjoying all the things I really loved (a.k.a. my vices). I had to give up beer and food that I craved for long periods of time to reach my goals. I believed then and still believe now, that there is nothing wrong with the occasional beer session and some "good for your soul" food. The difference between now and my 20's is that I enjoy my beer and rich food less frequently. I gave my eating style the 80/20 rule a few years back when I started to notice that if

I brought a healthier breakfast and lunch to work, and only ate dinner out, I would lose a few pounds here and there. Most importantly I would keep it off. Ironically, at the time when I noticed this change, I was unaware that I was following the Pareto Principle. The principle generally correlates to my rule in that if 80% of my meals were healthy, then the negative effects of the other 20% of unhealthy meals were more limited. Later, in my healthy eating I moved my eating out to only Friday and Saturday night. Not only did I have more money in my checking account, I was steadily losing some of the lineman weight. Nothing was really drastic because I was still eating breakfast and lunch with a little southern covering, but at least I was preparing most of my meals, which means I controlled the content.

I do not want to get in the weeds about diets and eating. There are plenty of good books that doctors and nutritionist that have written books that can set your eating regimen up with all the correct nutrition for your cholesterol make over. What I want to convey is that it is possible to be successful in losing weight and becoming a healthier you for the long term if you start to think about eating in this way:

- 80% of the time eat what is good for you and 20% of the time eat what is good for your soul.

I equate that formula to "eat what you want" for 2 meals a week. I save those for when I go out to dinner or when I cook for family and friends. It still takes discipline to pass up the morning donuts in the break room or the quick burger and fries, but at least I can look forward to Mexican on Wednesday nights and a Gastro Pub on Saturday night without worrying about my waistline or arteries.

The crazy thing about food is you need it to operate your body. Too much of the wrong kind of food, over a long period of time, it will cause your body to fail. But if at some stage of your life before the point of "No Return", if you start eating what is right for your body, it can and will recover to its full operating capacity.

Now that you are becoming a father, you have some external motivations to develop good eating habits. What you cook and eat will be observed by your kids and will carry on with them into adulthood. Trust me, it was hard to understand why cooking my vegetables in vegetable oil was not necessarily a good way of eating. Imagine if your kids never had to consult a doctor about weight, diabetes, cholesterol, or other weight related maladies because their father and mother showed them how to live a healthy lifestyle. That is a legacy worth living. If you start during the pregnancy, you will have multiple weeks to fail and adjust. Remember if you are eating meals in the 80/20 rule for more than 90 days it will become the way you eat the rest of your life unless you consciously choose otherwise. If you started reverting back to your old ways, you will be very aware if you did not meet the rule week over week. Keep this thought in mind, this not an extreme weight loss program designed for you to lose 50% of your body weight in a few months. My approach is a long game. Small incremental successes will eventually add up to a great change. If you start as soon as you find out your partner is pregnant, within the term of the pregnancy there will be a stark difference in your waistline. Within two years you will have to upgrade your wardrobe! It will also be just in time for you to start chasing your little track star around the yard.

Here are a few general tips to shopping and eating that might help you get going in the right direction. With a commitment to these tips I promise you will get great results:

Shopping Cart

1. Shop the perimeter of the store for all your major meals and snacks.

2. Fresh fruits and veggies: Eat as Much as you want

3. Fish and poultry: Keep it to 3 to 5 oz. portions per meal.

4. Beef and Pork: I would limit these two meats to one meal a month. Get premium cuts and grass fed. You will find that the meat is much more flavorful than the standard beef and pork sold in the store. Your local butcher shops can provide some quality cuts found in a typical grocery store for half the cost. Try to get grass fed and not grain fed meats because there are more nutrients in grass and acorns than cornmeal. Plus eating less beef and pork is better for the planet!

5. Bread - Whole grains from the bakery: Bread should be less than 20% of the total portion, or calories, of your meal unless you are working out on a regular basis. If you are doing high cardio workouts for over 45 minutes you could make the carbs around 35% of the meal on work out days. Sour Dough Bread is the best bread because it has a good glycemic index. For your information, the glycemic index (GI) is a ranking of carbohydrates/sugars on a scale from 0 to 100 according to the extent to which they raise blood sugar levels after eating. Foods with a high GI are those which are rapidly digested and absorbed and result in marked fluctuations in blood sugar levels. Low-GI foods, by virtue of their slow digestion and absorption, produce gradual rises in blood sugar and insulin levels, and have proven benefits for health. Low GI diets also reduce insulin levels and prevents insulin resistance. (www.gylcemicindex.com)

Eating Regimen

Eat Breakfast when you are actually hungry. Most of the time when we wake up the "hungry" sensation we are feeling is our bodies way of saying we are thirsty. Instead of slamming a cream cheese bagel or a bowl of heart healthy cereal, chug 12-15 ounces of water with a fresh squeezed lemon. If you are still feeling that hunger sensation 1 hour later, then eat a good protein laden breakfast. To keep from having to interpret your stomachs signals, I suggest sticking to timing your first meal to 12 to 15 hours after your last meal, a.k.a. Intermittent Fasting (IF). Below is the general strategy for IF eating regimen.

- Make breakfast a nutritious meal with all food groups. My favorite breakfast is 1 boiled egg, ½ an avocado, ½ of a tomato, and 1 apple.

- Eating breakfast 12 hours later means that you should not eat after 8 P.M. on a regular basis. If you have to eat late, make sure there are no carbs or sugars in the meal. Studies have shown that late night carbs increase heartburn, fat storage, and restless sleep. I was a case study for the fat storage results. If you eat later than 8 P.M. because of work or other commitments, breakfast might not be necessary. If you hit 12 to 15 hours around 10 A.M. and take lunch at 12 noon, I recommend eating fruit only for your breakfast. So, if your last meal of the day is after 8 pm, make lunch the next day the first full

149

serving meal. Your body will recognize that is going to get the food it needs so it will not go into survival mode.

Following an IF plan is not as hard as it seems. As long as you go to bed at a reasonable time, you will be sleeping through most of the fast. Remember, if you wake up and your stomach is growling, start the morning with a quart of water with a splash of lemon. You will find the morning hunger will subside quickly. If you are a coffee drinker, you are in luck because caffeine is a natural appetite suppressant. Coffee will get you over the mid-morning hump when real hunger growling is occurring. My experience with IF is that I wake up feeling fresh and light. Most of all, my brain is on fire, so I do some of my best work in the mornings.

- Snack midafternoon with fruit and nuts. Keeps the nuts to about a ¼ cup. Be careful with snacks. They can add up quickly. Here are some links to articles that outline the health risks associated with snacking and late-night treats:

  - https://www.theatlantic.com/health/archive/2012/06/why-late-night-snacking-is-bad-for-you/259085/
  - https://www.nytimes.com/2014/10/26/opinion/sunday/the-dangers-of-eating-late-at-night.html?_r=0

Metabolic Rate

There is one other action you can take to help fine tune eating habits. Everybody needs to determine how many calories their body needs to thrive. Weight Watchers and your doctor tend to use BMI as their baseline for health. In my opinion, BMI is not a great guide to health. Here is why: If a man walked into Weight Watchers or doctor's office and was measured to be 6'-5 and 250 lbs. the BMI chart would indicate that person was morbidly obese. But if that man happened to be JJ Watt or Ray Lewis who are at 250 lbs. and 8% body fat on any given Sunday, then I would say the BMI and Weight Watchers charts are severely flawed. BMI does not account for muscle mass or bone density. Good news is that technology is providing us other options to determine your caloric need and the status of your health based on weight. In most cities there are sports doctors that typically either have a water tank or Body Pod. These two devices will measure your muscle, fat, bone, organ, and water weight separately. If these options are not available there are less accurate home scales that will provide the data. Once the mass of your muscle is determined a quick ratio can be applied to the results and spit out what calories your muscles need to thrive. (Usually 11 to 14 calories per pound of lean muscle) The sports doctor will provide you all the information, but generally if you are over 35% body fat you are really out of shape. If you are between 18% and 22% you are really healthy. For this discussion, the most important metric in the test is the body's required caloric expenditure known as Base Metabolic Rate (BMR). Your BMR is based on your muscle mass only. Once you know your BMR and you apply the caloric value to the 80/20 rule, you will lose unneeded weight quickly, not be so hungry, and have ample energy for daily activities. Your BMR is also necessary to know if you are following the IF method to lose weight so that you consume the daily. calories your body needs. Please note that most fitness apps use BMI as the basis of calorie intake, but you can set them up to monitor calories based on your BMR instead of BMI.

Because you and your partner are on this journey together, it is essential that you practice the 80/20 rule together. If only one of you is eating well regularly and the other keeps filling the pantry with sweet cakes and potato chips, the chance of your success is going to diminish. A human's will power is only so strong!

As you know by now being a Daddy Doula is mostly about generating a connection. In my house nothing creates a better opportunity for bonding than cooking a great meal, or any meal, with my wife. Sometimes we even get to do the shopping together which can be its own adventure when you are cooking a new recipe that requires some unusual ingredients. But like many of you, finding time to cook extravagant meals can be hard so I want to provide a few tips that can ease some of the pain and hassle of eating well over the long haul of a busy work week.

1. Using online shopping carts. You end up buying only what you need and those "special" treats stay out of your

basket.

2. Grocery delivery services are great to save time.

3. Invest in some glass storage bowls. For one, they are reusable. And two, you can heat up your saved meals in a microwave without worrying about transferring chemicals from the plastic storage bowl to your food. Have you ever wondered why your plastic bowls are always stained after your heat up some left-over spaghetti? The sauce moved into the plastic and plastic moved into the food.

4. Try to pre-cook an assortment of meats and vegetables in one cooking extravaganza.

5. Grill or bake enough chicken breasts, pork chops, and turkey sausage with an assortment of flavors for at least 4 lunches and 4 dinners. I like premade Italian and Cajun seasonings, along with salt, pepper, and garlic, to create my flavor profiles. Cooked refrigerated food will last without issue for about 4 days.

6. I would cook fish before the meal because they can get chewy if microwaved.

7. Beef can be cooked on the day of because it is so good when it comes sizzling off the grill.

8. Create 8-10 bowls of thick chopped raw veggies. Add salt, pepper, and little garlic to each dish. Right before you

microwave the dish, add a little water and olive oil. Delicious steamed perfection.

9. If you have a sweet tooth after a meal, baked cinnamon apples and baked grapefruit are great options to throw in the oven while you are eating. Sprinkle some Stevia to add some additional sweetness if needed.

10. Create packets of heart healthy snacks with sealable bags that are easy to grab and take when on the go. I would create snacks that are sweet, savory, and filling like a salted nut mix with dried fruit. Throw some chocolate chunks into a few of the packs for your partner to make her snacks a little more satisfying. She will want food throughout the day during the pregnancy, so a good hearty snack will help her battle cravings for high-fat sugary snacks. As I said before, be mindful of the snacks. The calories can add up quickly and you want to stick close to your BMR.

It might seem obvious, but the better-quality food your partner eats on a regular basis, the healthier she and the baby will be in the long run. The baby is in a symbiotic relationship with the mother while in the womb. The sugars and nutrients that she eats will be transferred to the baby.

Nutritious Food = Healthy Mom = Healthy Baby

In my opinion, a person's eating habits is the leading indicator of their overall health. If you eat fast food regularly you are most likely overweight. If you eat fruits and vegetables with every meal you are most likely not a health risk. By following the 80/20 rule, along with consuming the proper caloric value based on your BMR over a few years, you will find yourself in a very healthy position. The gut and flab will slowly melt away. Hopefully, if you choose to break the 80/20 rule and are eating some high calorie, fat laden, sugar filled yumminess, it is because you did a crazy 1000 calorie work out that morning. That is right, a little exercise in the mix can almost negate the 20% of bad food you eat, and you will speed up the weight loss process. You don't have to exercise like a professional athlete to become healthy if your general diet is sound. All though exercise has long lasting effects that will keep muscles strong, lean, and more durable, while making the bones strong, for the later years of life when you want to wrestle with your grand kids in the back yard.

Chapter 6.2:
Slow Start Rule

From the time I could run as a boy to about 19 years old, I was outside playing in the woods building forts, playing capture the flag games, or playing sports. I never missed a day or a week without some sort of sustained activity. For me, college changed that routine. Instead of using the state-of-the-art workout facility on a regular basis that was provided by my school, I started substituting activity days for hangovers. And over a few years, the activity days went to Zero and I ballooned to over 300 lbs. As mentioned before, at 30 I decided my weight was unacceptable. But there was one other factor I have not mentioned so far about my choice to become healthier. The same year that I made the decision for a healthier life, I blew my hamstring playing kickball. A former soccer player from age 4 to 20 I knew how to kick the ball. At 30 my new 300 lbs. body still knew how to kick the ball but did not know how to run with the additional weight. After a booming kick over the center fielder I found myself only at second base when he got to the ball. I had to pick up the pace to make it home, so I bore down like a drunken bull and rounded third. I hit a soft spot in the ground and heard a small pop. I tumbled into the ground about 10 feet short of home plate with an embarrassing thud. When the dust settled, I had a slightly torn hamstring and a crushed sense of my athleticism. I was no longer the athlete I used to be or currently the one I wanted to be. More importantly, there was no way that I could be the active dad that I wanted to be, especially if I was in my 40s and 50s when my not yet conceived kids would be hitting their limitless energetic stride.

After I recovered from my injury I was determined to get back into athletic shape. I knew part of that goal was to lose weight, so I tried some of the low carb fad diets concurrently with my own unqualified fitness program. The healthy eating and exercise trend were 1 week and done. After about 3 workouts I would be so sore that I couldn't walk without grunting, much less get my hands to my head to wash my hair. By the time I was able to do another work out, I had already reverted to bad eating so there was no reason to keep exercising. This cycle continued about every 4 weeks for about 6 months. I would get motivated, hit the diet and gym hard and fail again. It was probably on the fourth try, by pure brute force of self-assessment and ego check, that I got it right. I decided to forget the fad diets and try to eat a little better than fast food. I also decided to ease into the workout exercises. When I started round 4 of my healthy life transformations, I decided to set a goal to run a 5k and do it in less than 35 minutes. That is by no means a formidable time, but it was a goal and I gave myself 3 months to train. At first, I would run for 2 minutes, walk 1 minute, and run 2 minutes until I reached 1 mile. I ran twice a week. I would throw in some pushups and sit ups to round out the work-out (3 sets of 10). After about 2 weeks I bumped the interval running up to 1.5 miles, along with bumping the reps up for the push-ups and sit-ups. I did this for 3 months and the craziest thing happened. Not only did I lose a few pounds and run the 5k in 32 minutes, I kept on working out after the race. In the last 10 years I have never gone one week without running or exercising at least one day in a week. Exercise has become a part of the routine of my life so much that my Thanksgiving and Christmas day workouts are part of the family holiday traditions.

I want you to start exercising on a regular basis and I want you to be successful. But what I do not want to happen is for you to fail as many times as I did before you get it right. I want exercise to become a lifestyle for you, so I need you to get to 90 days of constant exercise and activity. The only way I know how to do that is to set some milestones and for you to go slow in the beginning. The Slow Start rule is basically this: Start exercising today and give yourself a few extra reps and minutes every week. Eventually you will be able to sustain a 45 to 60-minute workout and feel great about it.

To get started you really don't need a gym. Instead you can try a few of these free activities:

1. Become a tourist in your own town. Park the car and visit all the hidden gems on foot.
2. Ride your bike around the park or maybe to a nearby town to have lunch (say 20 miles).
3. Visit your local elementary school and play on the jungle gym. Those monkey bars are harder than you think!
4. Hike the trails of your local state park. There are hidden jewels in most of them. Plus, nature tends to re-center

our spirits to the beauty all around.

Most of the activities above are low impact so include your partner in the activity no matter what stage of the pregnancy. Free Day Dates! I feel the exercise connection coming!

Working Out with Momma

Before we move into your fitness revolution, I want to remind you that if you and your partner workout together, not only will you hold each other accountable to your goals, but you will also build that team bond that forms when you battle together. I want to warn you about this partnership, sometimes working out together might be frustrating, especially if you have different approaches to fitness. For me it is hard to workout with my wife. It is not that she can't do the same exercises; it is more that I am too much of a coach telling her how to do the exercises for us to enjoy the time. We also have different motivations for working out. Typically, I am interested in pushing myself to the limit so that I can return to the athletic me, whereas she just wants to exercise to be active. Before the first pregnancy we found a good solution to working-out together, we did Cross Fit® together for one month. If you are not familiar with Cross Fit®, it basically is Olympic lifting mixed with cardio that will train you to be a complete bad ass athlete. It is not for beginners. One of the good principles of Cross Fit® is that they provide professional coaches and proven workouts. We were there in the same puddles of sweat but doing it at our own pace. It was great. I was also very impressed with what she could do by the end of the 4 weeks. We stopped going when I got hurt trying to perform a handstand push-up. The aforementioned lineman status had not quite been overcome by this point, so it was a mistake to attempt such a move. After my recovery, we still wanted to work out together, so we found classes like Body Pump, Kick Boxing, and Spin that were offered by the local gym. When my wife found out she was pregnant, these classes provided avenues for us to keep working out together that were a little less intense. Your partner should be able to do most of the workout classes provided in a gym for the entirety of the pregnancy. Obviously consult with the doctor in case there are risks associated with the pregnancy. The workouts I provided later in this chapter include a little too much jumping for a pregnant woman so she might want to avoid these routines. If a gym membership is not in the budget or classes are not available, at least PLEASE, PLEASE, PLEASE walk with your partner at least 3 days a week for a couple of miles. Not only is walking a great exercise for a pregnant woman that generally promotes health, it is nearly impossible not to connect to her during your stroll. You can talk about work, religion, politics, dreams, future vacations, and even baby stuff. I find that challenging conversations make the walks more entertaining.

In the beginning of your pregnancy walks with challenging conversation will seem awkward if you have never really had one with your partner. For me, I have been lucky to have friends that enjoyed having challenging conversations. I found that over time these stimulating conversations made my friendships strong and resilient. When my wife and I started having these mind stretching walks, I had to learn how to navigate the unamicable topics without creating a gap in our relationship. But even where there was tension in topics like child discipline, at the end of the walk there was a deeper connection and appreciation for wanting to work through the tough topics. Once your conversations go beyond weather, traffic, and celebrity gossip and you start to tell each other your fears and excitements about being parents, your connection will grow exponentially. No matter how difficult the topic, you have 7 to 9 months to work out the details of your parenting philosophy. There are lots of great books out there on parenting and discipline. Pick out some books and read them together. I found that these books were helpful in helping us create a baseline approach to our parenting style:

1. Janet Lansbury – No Bad Kids: Toddler Discipline Without Shame

2. Dr. James Dobson – The New Strong Willed Child

3. Noel Janis-Norton - Calmer Easier Happier Parenting

On your walks you can talk about how amazing, or crazy and unrealistic, the author approaches parenting. The two of you can create a plan on how you are going to talk to your kids and how you will discipline. Even if you don't agree with the author, at least you will expose yourself to alternative methods where you can compare your proposed parenting style for its own merits and weakness. I believe that parenting discussions are essential to have prior to D-

Day. You and your partner need to have your philosophical points decided on before you start raising your child. By the way, parenting will change as child ages and is influenced by the child.

If you are reading this book at least your partner will know that you want to be more informed about the pregnancy. Take it another step and read up on parenting. It never hurts to have some professional advice from family counselors and child psychologists who have published their findings in a self-help book.

Daddy Doula Workouts

The previous sections of this chapter have focused on getting you ready for the mental challenges of labor and delivery. The Momma Workout section was designed to get both of you moving and for creating another avenue to help you become more connected to her and the pregnancy. The Daddy Doula Workouts is about getting you strong and fit. If your partner is cleared by the doctors for moderate to intense style workouts, then you should invite her to join in on the sweat inducing fun. Before you get scared and cower back to the couch because the dollar signs are ringing up in your mental cash register, my approach to fitness does not require a state-of-the-art gym or hundreds of dollars in exercise equipment. You will be able to succeed with equipment such as resistance bands and light to medium weight dumb-bells, 10 lbs. to 35 lbs. You can usually find the dumbbells at springtime garage sales where people are selling their New Year's fitness resolutions at discount prices. Also, if you like having a coach to motivate you, there are many great exercise videos with routines that can get you into shape quickly. I caution using some of these videos from the start because they will take you from zero to 100 miles per hour, and within week one you will be in so much pain and unproductive in other parts of your life, you might as well have not started them. But I would suggest that you set some of these more intense workouts as a goal. I completed Beach Body's Insanity® and P90X® after about 3 months of running, pushups, and sit ups. After about

1 year of continuous exercise and really pushing myself, I was fit enough to run in a 5 mile- 28 obstacle Spartan Sprint®. Looking back from when I rounded third base and started down this new healthy lifestyle, I am now over 40 years old, finished the 15-mile 80 obstacle Spartan BEAST. So be encouraged. If I can get back to some semblance of the athleticism in my glory years, so can you Daddy Doula.

To help you commence the first steps to a new way of exercising I have laid out a couple of workout plans in the back of the book in Appendix A. You can visit my website at www.daddydoulaish.com for the worksheets. In this chapter I have set some goals or milestones for you to gauge your fitness level. I find that knowing your base line helps set goals. Goals are good motivators if you have a plan in place to help achieve them. Once you can reach the milestones I have provided below, you will be ready to take it to the next level of extreme training if you want. If extreme training doesn't sound like your cup of mojo, at least you know you will have a strong foundation to maintain until you are too old to care. A little caution from experience, meeting the milestone on your first try does not mean that you are ready to move to the next level if you can't walk, sit, or wave your hands without taking 1000 mg of Ibuprofen. But you would be closer than some.

Below are your milestones. The first work out inn your Daddy Doula training program is to determine your current athletic status.

Fitness Milestones			
Exercise	Reps/Distance	Goal Duration	Current Duration
Running/Walking	1.5 Miles	15 Minutes	
No weight Squats	50 Reps	1 Minute	
Push Ups	30 Reps	1 Minute	
Pull Ups	10 Reps	1 Minute	
Sit Ups	60 Reps	1 Minute	

The workouts I have put together in Appendix A and on my website are basic, but each will provide you with great results. If you are eating following the 80/20 rule you will see results fast. The program is intended to be slow. If you have not exercised in years, slow is the way to go to make sure you will keep coming back. Some early success will be great for your confidence. My goal is to get you exercising 3 days a week and being active every day. And what I mean by active is doing something that gets your heart rate above 100 bpm (beats per minute). An activity could be as simple as a one-mile walk, cutting the grass, and cleaning your house. In the end, if you get in a few good workouts in a week and are active every day you will easily hit all the milestones above in a very short period of time.

The workouts that I have created based on my experiences with Beach Body® programs, cross-fit, and playing soccer. I have catered them to the Slow Start Rule to help beginners. Your partner can participate in the routines for almost the duration of the pregnancy. In third trimester she might need to refrain from the jumping exercise and just do lower impact motion. If you are already a fit machine, I challenge you to complete the routines faster than the allotted time!

To help you understand the names of the exercises in the work outs, I am going to define each one so that you will know how to do each one.

Work Out Definitions:

Warm Up

Butt Kicks – running in place while making sure the heels of your foot hit the back of your leg. Modification is just to jog in place.

High Knees – running in place while bringing your knees up to same level as your waist. The modification here is to march in place while bringing your knees up.

Jumping Jacks – First motion is to jump while bringing your hands above your head and simultaneously spreading your feet to just outside shoulder width. Second motion is to jump and bring your hands down to your side while bringing your feet together. The modification here is to not jump but just step one foot to the side while raising your hands.

Side to Side Floor Touches – First motion is to skip left go into a side lunge and touch the floor. Reverse the motion while you swing your hands above your head and skip right into a lung and touch the floor. Modification here is to minimize your lung depth and don't touch the floor.

Stretches

Hamstring Stretch – Off set your right foot to the front of your stance about 12 inches. Transfer your weight to the front right foot and reach for your toes. Reach until you feel you right hamstring burn. Over the 30 seconds try and get deeper into the stretch. Switch legs.

Groin Stretch – Off set your right foot to the side of your stance about half your body length. Make sure both feet are parallel. Squat down until you feel the left groin engage. Over the 30 seconds try and get deeper into the stretch. Switch legs.

Calves Stretch– Push Up Position then walk your feet to your hands until in a "V" shape. Force your heels to the ground. You can rotate feet or do both simultaneously.

Quad Stretch – Move right heel to your butt and grab your ankle and pull up. If you need a chair for balance, use other hand to hold yourself in place. Switch legs after 30 Seconds.

Front Dive/Back dive – Stand with feet at shoulder width apart. Reach down for your toes in arching motion. (Front Dive). Reverse the motion swing your hands above your head and arch your back. (Back Dive) Hold at each front and back position for 2 seconds.

Scissor Arms – Stand with feet at shoulder width apart. Take your right arm and pull it across your chest keeping your wrist down and at same elevation of the shoulder. Take your left arm and squeeze your right arm to your chest. Switch after 30 seconds.

Exercises

Push Ups – belly on the floor, toes down and hands just outside of your shoulders even with the center of your chest. Suck in your stomach and push up. Keep a straight line between your head and your heels. Do not arch your back. Release and return to the ground, but stop once your elbows are at 90 degrees. Your Thumbs should be close to your nipples. Modification here is to place your knees on the ground to eliminate some of your body weight.

Power Jacks – Same as a jumping jack except your feet go out past your shoulders and you squat to legs form 90-degree angle. Then jump back to starting position with feet together and hands at side.

Suicide Sprints – Pick a point out in front of you about 5 yards. Run to the spot and reach down and touch it with your right hand. Run back to the starting point and touch with your left hand. For speed you almost jump into a lunge at end to touch floor while rotating so that you are facing the opposite direction.

Jump Knees – Start with feet shoulder width apart. Jump while bringing your knees to the same elevation as your waist. Jump as fast as you can.

Power Knees – Start with feet just outside of shoulder. Bring right knee up and across body to waist elevation. Rotate torso so that left elbow touches the right knee. Bring foot back to original position. Repeat as fast as you can. Alternating right and left feet/elbows.

Pogo – Start with feet together. Transfer all wait to right foot. Begin jumping on one foot. Switch feet after 30 seconds.

Fast Feat to Jump Turns – Start with your feet just outside of shoulder. Start running in place like a football player. After 5 seconds, jump and rotate to face the other direction. Feet should land relatively in same location. Repeat jump every 5 seconds.

Basketball Shots – You are simulating receiving a pass and immediately going up for the long three-point shot. Start off by shooting with your right hand and facing right. Switch hands and direction after 30 seconds.

Ice Skaters – You are simulating a speed skater. Start with your feet together place all your weight onto your right foot. Lean over like you are about to start a sprint. Jump laterally about half your body length and land on your left foot. Keep your left knee above your left foot and keep your right foot off the ground by swinging it behind you. Then leap back to your right foot.

Plank – Start off by facing down and resting on elbows/forearms while legs are extended out from and you are balancing on both toes. Plank Right is to rotate onto the right elbow and right foot only. Plant left is to rotate onto the left elbow and left foot only.

Mountain Climber– Assume "V" shape position. Bring right knee to chest then return foot to ground. Then bring left knee to chest then return to foot to ground. Repeat like you are running.

Side Jacks – Hand above your head and feet shoulder width apart. Bring right elbow down to meet your knee. Your knee should come up from the side and not to the front. Then repeat on your left side. Repeat as fast as possible.

Fast feet Burpee – Classic football drill. Quickly stamp your feet in place for 10 seconds then drop to bottom of push up position. Perform Push up, then jump feet to your hands, and then jump into the air. Repeat as quickly as you can.

Speed Jacks– Jumping jacks as fast as you can.

Low Squat Jabs– Feet just outside shoulders and lower into low squat position. Legs are at about 45 degrees. Elbows cocked at your side; hands fisted with wrists up. Throw a right jab while rotating fist so wrist rotates down and then return to cocked position. Repeat left side. Repeat jabs as fast as possible.

Speed Bag – Feet just outside shoulders and lower into low squat position. Legs are at about 45 degrees. Hands are fisted and in front of your face. Rotate like you are hitting a speed bag like Rocky Balboa.

Push Up Jacks – Assume push up position but start from the top. Feet should be together. Drop down while simultaneously spreading your feet to form a "Y". Push up and then bring your feet back together.

Back Flies – Feet together and drop your knees so that your legs form a 45-degree angle. Slightly bend over your knees but keep your back straight and head looking straight ahead. Arms should be in hanging down holding the dumbbells around your knees. Start pulling your arms out and back like you are trying to fly and then return your hands to the start position. Try to keep your wrists facing down when at the high point of the motion.

Shoulder Press – Place dumbbells on shoulders so your wrists are facing your ears. Press up while rotating your wrists to face out and then bring back to start position.

Curls – Stand tall and hold the dumbbells at your side. Press your elbows against your side and curl up until the weight hits your bicep. Return to start position.

Crunchy Frogs – Sit on your butt with knees at your chest. Wrap your arms around your legs. Lean back and throw your feet out in front of you keeping your back and feet off the ground. Return back to original position.

Toe Touches – Lay down on your back with feet out and hands above your head. Move toes and hands above your waist forming a "V".

I had a coach that believed you should always practice throwing, kicking, pushing, jumping, and sliding with perfect form. His philosophy was based on preventing injury and ensuring that you maximized the power and strength of the appropriate muscle groups. If you practiced perfect form all the time, no matter the success rate during practice, at game time you would be successful.

For the exercises I provided you, and any other you learn along the way, it is important that you do each one with perfect form. If you must squirm, kick, thrust, or whatever other poor form your body wants to do to get that extra rep, do not perform the rep. You will get hurt eventually. There are several modifications to most exercise to reduce the effort required. If you keep the required form, you will strengthen the primary muscles you are targeting, as well as your core muscles.

Work Out #1: Cardio Starter

Cardio Starter will kick start your cardio health. The general concept of the workout comes from my days of training for soccer. It was always hard for me to come out of winter with good conditioning so when we started running in early spring, I would have to throw in many rounds of walking before I had the proper endurance to run a straight 6 to 8 miles. I have also found in my recent experience with CrossFit® that a good cardio base will set you up for better strength training rounds to build overall strength and endurance.

This work out might seem too simple, especially if you are an x-athlete. But take it from a former athlete, if you have been sitting on the couch playing Madden and MLB for the last 10 years living out the glory days of your avatar, it will kick your butt for at least a few weeks.

This workout may be tough in the beginning but stick with it for a few weeks. Every time you try it, increase the run interval time and decrease the number of times you walk. Your goal should be able to get to the point where you can run the entire 4 minutes without walking before moving onto the next work out. And if you are feeling strong and encouraged, feel free to lengthen the entire work out.

Work Out #2: Cardio Power

Cardio Power is designed for all levels of fitness. Basically, it is about doing as many reps in a round as you can in the allotted time. If you push yourself, you will puke. But if you just barley perform the workout, you will still break a sweat. Try to stay in the middle and incorporate this workout at least once a week into your routine. The workout is designed to have a warmup, the actual work out, and a cool down. The actual work out portion is broken into rounds. Use the Rounds as your markers for success. You can either reduce the time of each round or just do one round until you are able to sustain the time. The Go-Slow Rule would say that you should only increase your interval by 10 minutes every two weeks until you can complete the entire work out. Once you have mastered the time of each round, then your goal is to increase the number of reps for each round. A good way to track your progress is to journal your workouts. During the breaks record your reps so that the next time you perform the workout you can try to exceed

Work Out #3: Powerhouse

Powerhouse is also designed for all levels of fitness. It incorporates strength and cardio. Again, the work out is broken up into warm up, stretching, the actual work out, and cool down. The actual workout has rounds. The first round of exercises will build your overall strength because you are hitting all the major muscle groups. Then you continue to the cardio rounds where the muscle you just stressed will be in cardio mania. The philosophy here is to build your strength and activate that strength for a sustained amount of time. This type of working out is also known in Physics as horsepower. If applied with the right amount of effort, Powerhouse can dominate a professional athlete's engine. But again, in our case, use the Rounds as your markers for success. The Go-Slow Rule would say that you should only increase your interval by 10 minutes every two weeks until you can complete the entire work out. Once you have mastered the time, then your goal is to increase the number of reps for each round. Use your journal to record your success.

I hope that the routines I have provided have given you a glimpse into what you are capable of when it comes to your fitness. The average person will not be capable in the beginning to complete these work outs. With some dedication to your fitness and patience, you will find that by the time the baby starts it's decent into the world you will be able to walk, squat and massage your partner for hours without breaking a sweat. You will have the strength and endurance you need to be a great Daddy Doula.

Summary: Bringing Out Your Internal Doula

I hope the previous chapters were informative about the pregnancy and gave you a starting point to help you get connected to the pregnancy. The general theme about all the suggestions provided is spending quality time with your partner doing activities that are centered on her and the baby. Participation is truly the only way you will become connected to the pregnancy. I am sure there are other activities that you and your partner can create that will help create the connection that she desires. I guess the big question for you is, "If I do all these things, how do I know that I made the cut and the Daddy Doula position is mine?" For me, I knew the position was mine when we were about 3 weeks out from the due date, and she had never mentioned hiring a Doula since the initial discussion. Good luck! Just kidding. I am not going to leave you hanging here at this stage in your connection journey. There are a few more areas that you can work on that will help you secure the Daddy Doula job. If you master Words of Affirmation and Hands of Silk Stone, not only will you be the starter in the delivery room, you will probably be the best husband on the block.

Chapter 7:
Learning Words of Affirmation and Encouragement

Once your partner is in full-blown contractions, there is nothing anyone can do except to encourage her along until the baby is in her arms. In my opinion, "Encouragement" is where a Doula makes their money. Doulas have an inherent sweetness and a trustworthiness that gets the laboring woman to do what is ultimately best for the delivery process. Some are naturals and some have been trained. Hopefully by this point you have followed most of the suggestions in this book and your partner trusts you and you are more comfortable with the idea that you can be her Daddy Doula.

- Doula Qualification #1 = Trust → Check.
- Doula Qualification #2 = Sweetness → In-Progress

Unfortunately, I can't teach you true sweetness. However, I can teach you enough about what to say to help get your partner through labor. Just remember if you start to get grumpy because of fatigue or hunger, your tone will change and may show signs of irritation. For me when I started to hit my limit, I remembered my wife was actually doing all the work. Keep her efforts in mind and work on perfecting your sweet tone. Your warming words will encourage her to want to keep going even though she is in immense pain. As soon as she gives up, the epidural or other pain relief methods will come into play.

There is a great book called the "Five Love Languages" by Gary Chapman. I would encourage every couple to read this book early in your engagement or when you have committed to each other for the long haul. For the purpose of our mission in getting you to be at a "Sweet Doula" status, a quick synopsis of the book will do. In general, the premise of the book is that each of us responds differently to the love languages identified in its chapters. Each love language is our way of receiving and giving love. If your partner receives her love by "Words of affirmation" then she is going to be blown away after I provide you a couple of my affirming phrases. But even if her love language is not "Words" and is maybe "Gifts", she will still respond positively to you when you are being your better self.

Some of my best phrases are below. Each might seem over the top, but in reality, they are the truth. When you are watching her move through the labor process, I am sure you will find some other over the top phrases that will fit how you are feeling about her:

- "I have never met a woman so strong and powerful. Keep it up."
- "You are more powerful than you know. Keep going."
- "Wow. You are so beautiful right now."
- "I have always known that you could do what you put your heart and mind too."
- "You are being so amazing right now."

- "I know that you are experiencing a lot of pain. You are being so brave. "
- "You are doing great. You are a Rock Star!"
- "Dang girl! You're somethin' special with all that animal like yellin'." You gonna scare the girl next door! (in the voice of a redneck diva)

I would suggest coming up with a few one-liners that fit your partner's personality. You know her best and know what she will respond to. One thing that I never said but I discovered after the birth of our fist born, my wife was encouraging herself during the labor by telling herself "my mom did it with all three of her girls with no drugs. I can do this too!" In the months leading up to the birth, we talked with her mother about her labor experiences with her daughters. I think my wife's personal birth story gave her some deep internal fortitude that helped her through the really bad contractions that I could not offer. Even though this might be good information and motivation, I would never compare your partner to her mom while she was in the middle of a contraction.

The context of encouraging phrases is everything when trying to motivate someone. You would never say "way to go. You did a great job." right after your kid struck out looking with a runner on third, or missed the goal by 5 feet on a game winning penalty kick. Those were encouraging words, but not applied at the right time. The right thing to say would have been "I appreciate your effort up there. Next time, with a little more practice, you will put that ball in play."

The same timing applies to the labor process. You don't want to say "Great Job. Well done" after the first contraction. She has a long way to go before her job is done. You might want to rephrase it, "You are more powerful than you know. Keep going!"

The contractions will vary in their magnitude of time and pain at each stage: pre-labor, active labor, and transition. In pre-labor the contraction will be quick, uncomfortable like bad gas. (That is how my wife was describing how she was feeling when she didn't know she was actually having contractions). In active labor the contractions will vary in length, intensity and pain. When she is in transition, the contractions will be intense, powerful, and extremely painful. There is no way to describe an experience you have not physically experienced, but my wife would probably say something like "imagine someone is tearing you apart two minutes at a time". At each stage of labor your words of encouragement will have to change.

Pre-Labor

At this point you are a long way out. I would choose words that are getting your partner ready for the long haul. Patience, pride, and love would be the adjectives I would inject into your words. My favorite for Pre-Labor phrases are the following:

- "I have always known that you could do what you put your heart and mind to."

- "You did great during that one. You are going to make this labor thing look easy."

Active Labor

At this point you are most likely at the hospital or on the way. Here is where you have to give your partner the determination and the fortitude to complete the labor on her own and with no medical intervention. The contractions are intensely painful at this point and more frequent. I would choose words that are letting her know that she is capable. Strength, toughness, and amazement would be the adjectives I would inject into your words. My favorite phrases for Active Labor are the following:

- "Wow. You are so beautiful right now."

- "I know that you are experiencing a lot of pain. You are so brave. You are going to get through this".

- "I have always known that you could do what you put your heart and mind to."

- "This is what you want. In a few moments the wave will be over. Accept It and let it pass through you."

Transition Labor

If this is your first L&D, at the moment Transition starts you will most likely be way out of your element. Your partner is in lots of pain from the contractions forcing the baby down the birth canal;

her hip joints are dislocating, and uterus is expanding 4 times its original size. There is nothing she can do now to ease the pain. She is in the homestretch. The baby is crowning and almost here. It might seem that her mind will be occupied by other activities like pushing, but your partner will be searching for you both physically and emotionally. There will be no doubt when she is in transition labor so make sure you are by her side, have her by the hand, leg, or back and are reaffirming her efforts. Powerful and confirming would be the adjectives I would inject into your words. My favorite phrases for Transition Labor are the following:

- "I have never met a woman so strong and powerful. Keep it up."

- "You are so amazing. Keep going. In moments we will be meeting our baby."

- "I can see the head! You are so strong! You can do this!"

I am sure that you can use the phrases above as inspiration to create your own collection of "words of affirmation". Write them down and practice them on your partner to see how she reacts. During my wife's three labors I used many phrases. Some were horrible and others seemed to have done the trick. Below are a few basic observations I made during her labor that might help with creating your phrases and when to use them:

1. Have a positive attitude to the very end. If she scolds you or corrects you for something you said or did, try not to

get frustrated. You will be tired and emotions will be on edge so if she does comment about your efforts, don't get defensive and just apologize to her and move on. Remember she is the one that matters here. (I admit I had to apologize quite a few times!)

2. Listen to what she is saying. If you are trying to lighten the mood with some of your good-natured humor and she says something like "this is not the time to be funny", bite your lip and move on to your sweet words. Try again later. You might get one of those gut-wrenching laughs that you have been looking for your entire comedic life.

3. Be flexible. If she is not responding well, try different approaches: sweet, calming, drill sergeant, and silence are viable options for any contraction. You will just have to try and read the moment. If you guess wrong, apologize and sit silent until the contraction is over. Try another approach on the next contraction. There are plenty of contractions in the labor process. Batting over .300 would be a good average in my opinion.

When the contractions are at full tilt there is no telling what your partner might say. She might insult you, blame you for her pain, or ask you to get out of the room. If the situation gets this tense and uncomfortable, remember the contractions only last for a minute or two. Remember that she chose you to be her Daddy Doula and not her mom, sister, or the paid professional. Once the pain subsides, she will come to a more stable mental state, at least for a moment. In that moment, you must reassure her that you are on her team and that you are so proud of her efforts. Let her know you will be there by her side until the very end helping her where you can. Whatever you do, don't leave her alone because you are mad at her or your feelings are hurt! If you must collect yourself, make an excuse to leave her side momentarily. Let her know during one of the rest periods that you are heading to the bathroom or to refill your water bottle. I can almost guarantee when you come back after a couple of contractions alone with the nurse, she will be ready for you to resume your Daddy Doula duties. "Words of Affirmation" is going to be your number one tool in your Daddy Doula bag that will help your partner's mental strength during and after the contraction. So, it is important that you become an expert at empathy and communication if it is not in your natural tool bag.

Chapter 8:
Hands of Silk Stone

If "Words of Affirmation" and sweetness is just not your thing, you have one more tool in the Daddy Doula bag to master to help your partner have a vaginal unmedicated birth; that is massage. Once you have mastered massage, she will call you by your new name, Hands of Silk Stone. This is where your inherent man strength will help her body get through the labor. Yes, your strong, firm hands will be unleashed in a soothing and calming manor to help get her body to relax during and after the contractions. I have seen on the coupon sites some two- and three-day classes to learn basic massage techniques. I would enroll in one of these classes if you are a complete amateur masseuse. I admit that I never took a class. But one thing I learned over the years, either by osmosis or experimentation, was how to have the right amount of strength in my fingers while my hands glide around the shoulders and back. For me, becoming a Doula masseuse was not that big of deal because my wife has always said she loved my massages. I am not so confident in my abilities that I would turn down someone teaching me new techniques. When I have paid for a massage, I was mentally noting the pro's techniques and afterwards ask questions. In our Lamaze class I picked up a few massages that I added to my masseuse's tool bag that are specific for a pregnant woman. The new techniques made the class worth the time and cost. If you are nervous about your massage capabilities, don't worry I am going to give you all my secrets to massaging so that you can be the best Daddy Doula in the hospital!

Massage Tools

In every masseuse's tool bag, there are the basics: oils and massaging devices. The oils should not be sticky or leave a lasting residue. I would suggest the oil be slightly aromatic. Lavender is what the Ancients used in their topical oil and candle wax. It seemingly has natural relaxing properties. I do not believe those sentiments have ever been proven to actually work, but I do like the way Lavender smells. I would go with your partner to a local market store where artisans make oils specifically for relaxation and pick out a couple that she really likes. I guess for ease you can go to the big box bath stores where they have hundreds of choices, but what fun is that? No matter where the oil comes from, make sure that it does not irritate her skin and that your fingers can glide effortlessly when applying some compression and either readily absorbs or evaporates.

I would also recommend a massage tool to accompany the oil. These tools can be used for marathon massaging, as in labor massaging, to give your hands a break when needed. There are hundreds of infomercial products out there, so you will have many choices. Out of all the shapes, sizes, gismos, and wackadoodles, I would recommend the following properties in a massage tool:

1. It is small enough to fit in your hand

2.   It rolls or glides as you push it.

3.   Vibrator is okay as long as you can turn it off

When you combine the oil and massage tool with a few of my techniques, you will have all that you need to help relax and soothe your partner during and in-between her contractions. You can also use them after the baby is here when she needs a little R&R.

General Massage Techniques

Most likely your partner is either going to be sitting in a chair, kneeling on all fours, or standing when she is in labor. She will never be in the traditional massage position lying on her stomach with her head through an opening. The reason is obvious, so you will have to adjust your mind set when it comes to massaging her.

Most massages you pay for in a spa are thirty minutes to an hour in duration. But for that masseuse, you are most likely not their only customer for the day. You might be the 4th or 5th person.

> *Question*: So how does a masseuse massage for so many consecutive hours?

> *Answer*: They use gravity.

Using gravity is the first general rule for marathon massaging. When you are applying compression while circling your hands, thumbs, and fingers around your partner's back, put some of your weight into your efforts. If you position yourself so that you are above her, the slightest change in angle, can add just the right amount of force to your fingers that will make her muscles melt under you.

It takes years to get your hands and fingers strong enough to massage for hours on end. You don't have that long of a training period, so you will need to apply the second general rule for marathon massaging: use your fists and forearms regularly. When you gently place your fists in your partner's lower back and move them around in small circles, she will think she is in that massage chair at the mall. You can either use rule one or your brute strength to vary the pressure of the massage. Either way, your fists will seem like silk stones are gliding across her back when used in conjunction with the oil. When the hands begin to fail, don't be afraid to reach into your Go Bag for a Massage Tool. These little pleasure devices can give your appendages some well-deserved rest after a few hours of Pre-Labor massaging.

I have a few go-to massage techniques that I use for general pleasure applications. The next sections will provide some specific techniques to apply during Pre and Active Labor, or anytime you want to melt your partners stress away.

Shoulder Dough

Shoulder Dough Technique is my primary move. When applied correctly, you can literally make her knees buckle. The technique can be applied when she is sitting or standing. Your thumbs are the key here. I can only last about 15 consecutive minutes on this technique because it is all hand strength. So, the general technique is like it sounds, you are going to knead the shoulders (traps) like you would bread dough. Place your partner's trapezius muscle (trap)between your thumb and fingers. The thumb should be on the back of the trap and fingers on the front of the trap. Apply pressure with your thumb and slowly roll it in circles while simultaneously squeezing your fingers. Release the pressure between your thumb and fingers with a slight rhythm. Move your thumb and fingers in towards the neck and repeat the squeeze. When at the neck, roll your thumbs around the back of the neck. The thumb pressure at the neck should be lighter than when at the back of the trap. Once you give the neck a little love, move out towards the shoulders. When at the shoulders, give them a full handed squeeze. Get your fingers and thumbs into rhythm. Keep changing the angle of your thumb on the traps: high, low, middle, top. Just keep rolling and squeezing. Sometimes she will like harder squeezes and other times lighter. You will know what she wants by her body tension. If your thumbs start to get tired, rotate them up to the top of the traps and use the heel of your hand. This actually gives the front of the trap some extra attention because your fingers will dig in a little more.

Spider Fingers

This move is fun and a giggle getter. Basically, it is "itsy-bitsy spider" with more pressure. Your partner's entire back is going to be a playground. I like to start at the lower back. Put your right index finger and middle finger to the right of her spine. Similarly place your left index finger and middle finger to the left of the spine. Apply pressure on all fingers and begin walking your fingers up the back just staying to the outside of the spinal column. At first, I like to go all the way up to the shoulder blades and roll out towards the sides. Give the lats a good squeeze while you are there. On the third or fourth spider walk I go all the way up the back of the neck. When you get to the base of the neck you will have to reduce the pressure. The muscles in that area are smaller and not as taut. Since you are the spider walking you can vary the length of your finger travel from small strides to long strides. You can also vary the pace of your finger walk from slow to quick.

In the beginning you go can for a long-exaggerated strut, like the Pimpin' daddy you are, up and down the spinal boulevard. But to keep it fresh and to keep the nerves from literally ignoring the pressure, stopping those good feelings to your partner's brain, throw in some fast fingers. "Fast fingers" are really light and quick touches that move up, down, and all around her back and neck. This technique will almost always get some giggles and squirming.

Rolling Stone Fists

This is a professional move and requires knowing your strength and having some endurance for applying your strength. To know your own strength implies that you have strength. See the Slow Start Rule, for information on how to get ready for this massage technique. As the master Yoda says, "strength have you must" to be a great masseuse.

I would only deploy this technique on the large back surfaces, or the legs. If you start pressing on the bone with your knuckles, you may cause bruising.

To begin the technique, make sure your partner is in a position she can resist the pressure of your weight by sitting, benching on the ball, or standing up against a wall bracing with her arms. When she is not 9 months pregnant and does not have that sexy roundness up front, she can lay on her stomach. But if you want to prepare for the labor, I would practice with her on her side, leaning over the bed, in a chair, or using the yoga ball.

Next lather up her muscles with some of that fancy oil you purchased. You really want to be able to glide and press at the same time. To me the best spot for this massage is the lower back and the lats. To begin, make a fist and place each fist on either side of her spine. Put your thumb down pointing up the back so it is acting as another pressure point. Start to make small circles and then slowly begin adding pressure. Move around her lower back in small increments and make the circles slowly. Start moving around to her hips and buttocks. This might be a little unsettling to your partner if she is leaning against the bed because her butt is going to start jiggling. Use your affirming words here and make her feel comfortable and confident. Keep moving in small circles and slowly glide up the lats. If you don't have the advantage of gravity here, your pecs are going to start burning. To give them a break, slowly roll to your forearms and slide them back and forth over the lats like a master cellist. Once you have spent some time on the lats, hips, and buttocks, return to the lower back for the grand finale. At the lower back with both fist on either side of her spine, rotate your thumbs towards her shoulders. Slowly and firmly press more on your thumbs and begin moving up towards the shoulders. Once you get there, squeeze the shoulder like you learned in Shoulder Dough a few times and return down the back with thumbs pressing down. Again, if you are getting tired, the forearms can be used temporarily. Rolling Stone Fists technique will actually help the muscle relax. It is more of a deep tissue massage. You will not be able to keep going back to this technique at the same pressure because the muscle will begin to fatigue and not respond with pleasure signals. You will have to lighten your touch up to be more of a soothing massage.

Sweep the Legs

One the of the largest muscle groups on the body are on the legs: quadricep and hamstring. These muscles in combination are known for their power and endurance. When it comes to labor, legs are essential. Your partner will be walking and squatting, or maybe even running (if she is like Amber Miller) for the duration of the labor. The two of you will be making laps around the neighborhood during Pre-Labor and making laps around the hospital during Active-Labor. During Transition she will be squatting, crawling, and whatever else her instincts tell her is the best motion or position to be in. Her legs are going to be tired and aching. Yours will be too, but during the labor your complaints of soreness are of no concern to anyone. So, a nice leg massage would be a well needed treat.

Like before, this technique is best used with your partner lying on her stomach. But since you are practicing for labor, have your partner lean over the bed so that her legs are straight. Keep her knees slightly bent so the heart can move the blood from the legs back to the heart. If the legs are locked, she could pass out. Again, lather up the front and back of her legs from her heel to her groin with some good soothing oil. Because the legs are a larger muscle you are going to have to apply more pressure to get some results. You are also going to have to deploy multiple techniques to get this job done. The good news is you already have the best one for large muscle in your bag, Rolling Stone Fists. You are going to throw that one into the circuit when your fingers need a break from Sweeping the Leg.

Work one leg at a time. To get started spread your fingers out as far as you can. Place your hands on her upper leg so that your hands are wrapped around the single leg. Your thumbs should be in the middle of her hamstring and the fingers should be wrapped around to the quad. Your wrist will be at 5 o'clock and 7 o'clock. Start up high in the groin area and offset your hands so that the thumbs have a vertical separation of a few inches. Squeeze the thumbs and fingers and start sliding down the leg slowly. Go down through the knee to the ankle. When you get to the lower leg, there is not as much muscle in the front, so you can either relax the fingers or run the thumb down the calf, or you can keep going with the full hand. The first few times the lower leg will love the full hand. But eventually those 4th and 5th fingers will get tired. You can then just use the fingers as a brace to apply more pressure with the thumb. As you sweep the leg up and down, you can change your angle of approach to get more of the muscle. Rotate your alignment to 4 o'clock and 6 o'clock, and then 6 o'clock and 9 o'clock. When your fingers start to get tired, deploy your rolling stone fists. If your muscles are fading quickly, deploy one of the mechanical massaging tools. Sweeping the leg will provide your partner's legs immense pleasure and relief so it is a must have massage skill.

One of the biggest issues with the sweeping the legs is that you have to be down on the ground. At home I would put a yoga mat down so that I could rest on my knees. The mat provided enough relief for the practice rounds. In the labor room I used the nurse's stool to sit on. The stool was a Godsend because it seemed that sweeping the leg was our massage of choice for 2 of the 3 labors and pregnancies!

Now with massage techniques in your skill set, you might be asking when is the best time to deploy these techniques? The short answer, as soon as the first contractions start. Remember the more she relaxes during and after the contraction the more her uterus will widen to ultimately reduces her time in labor.

Combining Massage and Contraction Meditation!

A Daddy Doula can be like a Jedi if he deploys masterful massage techniques while doing mind control with Contraction Meditation. Recall In *Chapter 5.5 Yoga Balls, Contraction Meditation, and Visualization* that for every contraction there is a rest period. During that rest period you want to be maximizing the relaxation. So whatever body part you are verbally getting her to relax during the meditation you should also be massaging. Insert whatever massage technique or massage tool that she finds in that moment to give her relief. You will have to rotate techniques and areas of focus. I found that my wife preferred light touches instead of massage during her contractions. I assume she did not like the extra pressure. The only time more pressure was requested was in the last stages of active labor right before transition started.

Bonus Technique: Not for the weak!

When your partner is in the late stages of Active Labor and contractions are crushing her, you are going to be called upon for your strength. Sometimes that will be to hold her up while she is squatting. Other times, your strength will be needed when she is on all fours clenching in pain yelling for you to do something. I have one technique that you can provide in that exact moment. It is called the Quadra Power Vice. This is the money move when she is in those long contractions and her hips are beginning to readjust to make room for the baby in the birth canal. This is the hardest move in the book. You will only have to apply the move during late active labor. In the beginning it might be too much power, so you will have to utilize the move when your instincts tell you. Your partner will let you know to continue applying it. She might call on it and tell you to stop and go back to sweeping the leg. But when the moment is right, this move can provide her significant relief and will be called upon over and over again.

The Quadra Power Vice requires your partner to be on all fours or bending over holding on to something. If your partner is kneeling on the ground, make sure her knees are cushioned with a towel, or the yoga mat you packed in your Go Bag. (I will get to the Go Bag later, but just note this addition for now). You will have to be seated in a chair or on the yoga ball, unless your quads are so strong you can hold a skier's squat for 2 minutes for 100 sets. Once you are both in position, make sure her knees are lined up with her hips if kneeling on the ground. If she is standing up make sure her legs are not locked and feet are directly under her hips. You don't want them touching or spreading out like a frog. Place the palm of your hand on the outside of her hips, just above the joint. You should feel the muscle and a slight void between the muscle and the bone. Make sure the heels of your hands are in this groove. Your elbows should be out like an eagle with hands and forearms almost at a 90^0 angle. Now press your hands in and up. This move my friend is where all the pushups you have been doing for the last six months are going to pay dividends. Your pecs, shoulders, and triceps will burn to the inner depths of your muscle structure. If you are hitting the spot right and the contraction is in full tilt, your partner should feel a slight relief. Her muscles will not be doing all the work of spreading her hip structure out. Unless you are Bobby Beef Cake, this move will exhaust your chest and arms quickly. The move is called the Quadra Vice for a reason and is not for the "I forgot to do squats guy in the gym". "Quad" means four so the only other limbs you have left to bring into the configuration are your legs. Unfortunately, you won't be using your power muscles here; it will be all adductor muscles or your inner thigh area. So, either you can do ice skaters like the pros or borrow your mom's Thigh Master to get your adductors into peak fitness. To get the extra power needed for the Quadra-vice, place your elbows into the inner thigh close to your knee. When you begin pressing with your hands, squeeze your legs together against your elbows. You will be doubling your power and endurance. Trust me on this move. Learn it. Train for it. A deploy it!

All of the massage techniques provided above have been implemented in the labor room and verified for effectiveness by my wife to provide maximum relaxation. All you must do is figure out your special touch and the combination of the techniques that will unlock her tension. My advice is to listen to her moans, grunts, squirms, and silence to calibrate your personalized style. With a little strength training and practice you can become a better masseuse than the guy at the fancy spa charging her $100. You keep this kind of self-improvement up; you will have more money in your account and your partner will be bragging about your skills all around town!

Chapter 9:
Daddy Doula Go Bag

In some of the previous chapters I have referred to certain items that my wife and I utilized to help make her comfortable and to make the room more pleasant. There is a great tool that you will need to assemble in the last month of the pregnancy to help make you a professional Daddy Doula. The special tool I am referring to is often called the Go Bag. It is an assortment of items that you should pack into a bag or two that is specifically used for the hospital.

To make things easier for you, I am going to provide you a complete list of what you should bring and a reasonable explanation of why. I promise it will not be like going on a three-day trip that requires a full trunk of suitcases with five outfits a day. You should be able to put everything needed in one or two small suitcases that can be handled by you with ease. Below is my list of the essential items.

Birth Plan

Once you have detailed out your birth plan, you should print it and place into a strong manila envelope. The envelope should be put in a side pocket of the Go Bag. I would make a minimum of 4 copies of your birth plan. Make sure you use spell check prior to printing! For my wife and I the birth plan was the ice breaker for the nursing team. As soon as you arrive in the L&D room and start meeting the nursing staff, you should be shaking hands and passing your birthing game plan out to your nursing O-Line. In the event there is a shift change while you are in the middle of labor, your extra copies can be passes out to the relief team. If you have a good O-line, there will be notes on the original birth plan about milestones, decisions made, etc. The inscribed information on the birth plan can be passed along to the next shift so that there is a smaller gap in communication of your goals and progress.

Go Bag – Food and Nutrients

Energy Supplements

A basically understood rule about your role during the delivery of
your tiny titan is that you can only sleep when your partner sleeps.
This rule goes in line with there is to be no complaining about how
tired you are at any point in time. Unfortunate for you, there will
not be adrenalin being pumped into your blood stream every few
minutes from the pain of a contraction. You are going to need
another stimulant. The most common stimulant people take is
caffeine. And most people get their caffeine fix with a hot cup of
coffee. I have never been much of a coffee drinker, so I had to find
an alternative means of caffeinating. My go-to energy booster is a
pre-workout supplement. I use one that has taurine and green tea
extract in it to give a long-sustained energy boost that keeps you
alert. Instead of chugging it like you would before a workout, I sip
on it like a soda over an hour. There are other energy drinks on the
market that will do the trick. I would read the directions on the
bottles to make sure you don't exceed the number of recommend
servings for 24 hours. If your hair feels like it is growing and your
heart is pounding like a drum at a Five Finger Death Punch concert,
you might be a little over caffeinated. Whatever your choice of
stimulant, I highly recommend you do not drink coffee. Coffee has a
strong odor that not only comes from the cup, but from your
breath. You are going to be talking sweetly in your partner's ear
and the aroma of those gentle words during your meditation is

going to flow towards her nose. Sour Roasted Vanilla is not the smell that is going to bring her mind to a spot of peace and relaxation. Let's be honest here coffee drinkers, your breath stinks. I have never met a coffee drinker who did not have bad breath. So, if you must imbibe coffee, make sure you also have the next must have in your go bag.

Gum

Chewing gum is a good tool to keep you active. By its design, it provides you something to do to over and over. Gum will keep you sane over the long haul of labor plus it will keep your breath fresh while you are gently breathing your words of affirmation. I have heard that snipers chew gum to keep their minds focused when waiting for the target, so it probably would work for you in the L&D room.

Protein Bars and snacks

If you are like most men, we get grumpy and very stubborn when we are hungry. To avoid the Bruce Banner to Hulk Smash syndrome, bring lots of protein bars. The bars are very easily stowed and will last months, as long as you keep them at room temperature. The protein packed nutrition will also give you sustained energy for massaging and implementation of the Quadra Vice. I would also pack with the bars some dehydrated fruit snacks or gummies. This will give your taste buds a change-up.

Cash

In the event you get tired of the snacks you brought; I would store $10 to $20 worth of $1 bills in a side pocket. The cash can be used for vending machines in case the hospital cafeteria is closed.

Sports Bottle

I found that having the sports bottle, or a large thermos, was very efficient. I could store lots of fluids and as result I did not have to leave the room very often to refill. I purchased stainless steel thermoses because not only do they keep your drinks cold, they do not sweat moisture onto the tables or surrounding paperwork. My wife also had her thermos and straw for post labor recovery. During labor she was only allowed ice chips. In our Go Bag I threw in a little water enhancer to make her hydration more like a little sweet treat while she was nursing at 3 A.M.

Go Bag – Hospital Comfort

Yoga Mat

One of you, or even both of you, will be down on the ground during pre and active labor for different types of labor positions. Most hospitals are not carpeted for obvious reasons, so the yoga mat will provide some well needed cushion between the bones of the knee caps and the cold tile floors of the hospital when she is benching on the yoga ball or chair, or you are sweeping her legs during a great massage.

Massage Tools

If you forget your oils and massage tools, you are going to be working really hard keeping your partner relaxed. Put your favorite oils in a zip lock bag. Your massage tools should be placed in a location of the bag that is easily accessible. If you have been using it a lot during your massage practices, change out the batteries a few weeks before the expected D-Day.

Bedding for the Couch

Most birthing hospitals focus on making the mom comfortable and forget about the dad. If you are at a Gold Standard hospital, there will be a couch for the dad. But most will have some sort of reclining chair. I would seriously evaluate the sleeping options for you when considering the L&D hospital. But no matter the quality of the delivery hospital, you are not going to be sleeping in a plush hotel bed or chair. It will be stiff and plastic covered. So, to make your sleep as comfortable as possible, pack a bedding set like you are going camping. The yoga mat can act as the sleep pad, so don't be cheap on this purchase. Add a small down pillow, twin sheet set, and a small game-day blanket to complete the bedding set. If rolled and folded properly, these items can all fit in a medium sized duffle bag. Pack these items second so all the other items are on top. You might be able to add a small throw blanket that she likes to snuggle under, but she will have plenty of blankets.

Comfortable Clothes and Toiletries

If you are lucky, or with good planning, you will not be called away from work to meet your partner at the hospital when active labor starts. You will have time to get yourself dressed. If you can, I would sneak a good shower in before you head out to the hospital. You can take one together to help her relax through some of the early contractions before you hit the road to the hospital. But either way, when you leave, make sure you are in comfortable clothes, especially shoes. You are going to be in public so don't embarrass yourself with your favorite pajama bottoms or some other outfit that might give a little extra insight to the mystery of your manhood. I would stick to sporty attire: shorts, loose pants, and t- shirts. The hospital is going to be cold so select your apparel correctly. I am generally warm natured, so I wore shorts and a T-shirt even though it was 45^0 outside. Most hospitals have a 2 day stay requirement for deliveries. If there is a C-Section, it will be more time. I suggest packing 3 pairs of underwear and 3 T-shirts to change into at the end of each day. Include some toiletries like deodorant and baby powder. If there is a shower bring some soap. I would recommend the travel size to keep things small. You will also need to have one nice outfit for going home. The last day tends to be the moment lots of family are around and wanting to take pictures. Whatever your style, spruce it up a bit. These pictures will be on social media and on family fridges everywhere.

I hope you didn't forget your partner's clothes. Obviously let her pick them out. She only needs one or two nightgowns for the nights at the hospital. The hospital will be providing her special panties and gowns while she heals. But she will need an outfit during visitor hours and a going home outfit. Make sure she includes a small toiletry set that includes a small brush and make-up bag. You will have to set limits here. Some make up bags can be an entire duffle bag in of itself depending on your partner's glam tendencies. The whole point here is to grab one or two bags only so you will have to work with her.

But whatever you do, do not forget the going home outfit for the baby. No matter if it is a jersey for your favorite sports team or full-length gown, it goes in the bag as soon as it is purchased, washed, and dried (Always wash your kid's cloths before wearing to prevent skin irritation from chemical residues left behind in the clothing manufacturing)

There is nothing more to be said here about this topic so don't forget!

Go Bag – Baby Stuff

Baby Going Home Outfit

In case you already forgot, pack this outfit in the Go Bag as soon as it leaves the drier. Put it in a special compartment so that you can triple check that this special once in a lifetime outfit is packed before you head to the hospital.

Velcro Swaddles

For most first-time dads, you have no clue what a swaddle is or much less how to swaddle. It is a verb and noun. Confused? I was. Apparently, you can take a warm baby blanket and wrap a baby in it in such a way that gives the baby the tight sensation of the womb. There are some wraps, folds and tucks required to perform the perfect swaddle. If the baby looks like a mummy, then it is officially swaddled. The big question is, how long before the baby breaks out of the swaddle? If the swaddle is done properly, not even your little Hulk-a-manic can break out. But a poorly done swaddle can be compromised with one twitch of the arm. To avoid calling the nurse in every time the baby breaks free from your loose swaddle, pack some engineered swaddles. These little bags with Velcro seals will almost guarantee a few extra hours of sleep. The Velcro swaddles are so good, when your baby finally breaks free of them, they will literally be rolling over in their crib.

The Wedge

The wedge is another engineering tool to help you get a little extra sleep and keep your newborn safe. Some hospitals and doctors do not recommend their use because they do not like to have miscellaneous items in the crib with the baby. Use your best judgment. But when they are used and you have the proper swaddle engaged, the baby will be in a tight sleeve of warmth and have stability. Some babies like to naturally sleep on their backs and will not move all night. Others will tend to want to roll to their side. And when they roll, they startle themselves and wakeup a little mad. To keep the baby from rolling, the tringle foam wedges can be placed at the baby's hips. The wedges can be a great addition to the engineered swaddle to help keep the newborn stable. For the first few weeks you want the baby on its back, nose up and mouth open. You do not want the baby rolling over onto stomach and possibly suffocating in the sheet, or even risking SIDS (Sudden Infant Death Syndrome). Please refer to medical books or your doctor about more information on SIDS.

Go Bag - Entertainment

External Speaker and Music

There is nothing quite like the white noise of a hospital to put you to sleep or make 10 minutes seem like one hour. On the other hand, there is nothing like your favorite song suddenly streaming through the radio that will bring a smile to your face or take you to some other place in time. Music is a big part of relationships. I am sure over the course of dating and marriage you and your partner have agreed upon certain styles of music and certain artists. I would highly recommend you get a play list together that is between 4 to 8 hours that brings back good memories and is upbeat enough to keep the mood relaxed. With a lengthy play list, you can put your iPod® on random and just let it play. Make sure you have the power cords for your speaker and the music player. These days, most people have smart phones that can access Pandora® or Spotify® that will give you a great play list. If you start the play list while you are practicing your massages and relaxing techniques, after a few thumbs up and down, the play list will string together hours of great songs the two of you love. If you don't have the subscription for Pandora® or Spotify®, I would recommend signing up to eliminate commercials. There is nothing worse than when she is in a deep meditation while you are deploying the Sweep the Leg Technique when your least favorite sales guy enters your tranquil sound bubble through the speaker to advertise the best car deal in town that comes with bonus bucks.

The right music can set the mood of the entire delivery room. You and your partner will get into a nice rhythm during the contractions. The nurses and orderlies will also enjoy coming into your room where there are some good jams filling the normal stale silence of the hospital.

Books and Magazines

For the most part, during labor you will not have time to do much of anything except tend to your partner. But after the baby is born, there will be lots of down time for you, such as, between feedings. After each feeding it is likely Mom will be sleeping or being tended to by the medical team. There is really not much you can do except hold the baby, change diapers, swaddle, change diapers, swaddle, change diapers...... You get the rhythm. Between those new "life changing" tasks you can sleep or read. Watching TV is almost impossible because the room needs to be quiet for the baby to sleep and for the nurse to take readings on the baby and the mom. There is always your phone and/or tablet. You can stream movies and shows while listening through headphones, and of course update all your social media sites. I found these distractions to make me feel a little disconnected from my wife and baby because I could not hear the little sounds of life in the room. Instead I chose to read. Since I know that you are into becoming the better you, I challenge you to buy that 600-page book you have always wanted to read but never had time. There will be a news stand in the hospital so you will have plenty of magazines and books to choose from on the shelves. If you have never been much of reader, here is your chance to start. I have heard that your child will benefit from having parents that have books around that are being read. Most likely the child will pick up the same habit.

The Go Bag is the complete Daddy Doula Package and is the culmination of your preparation. The bag will establish your Daddy Doula certification. Think about it this way. When your circuit breaker gets fried after a lightning storm you have to call an electrician to come fix it. When the repair person shows up to the house, the first item carried by the electrician you probably notice is their tool bag. It is filled with black tape, meters, little light up doohickeys, wire cutters and a safety knife. Just like the electrician, the Daddy Doula is initially identified by his tool bag. And once your bag hits the L&D floor of the room and Birth Plan envelope is revealed to the medical staff, they will know that you and your partner are a team that has their act together.

Chapter 10:
Pulling it all Together: E.J., K.M., and J.J

The delivery of all three of my baby girls vaginally without an epidural; in short, what a ride! Childbirth is the ebb and flow of energy; it is constant changing emotions; it is a challenge to your mental fortitude. It is strength and endurance. The intensity of the experience is unimaginable. The elation of your heart and body when you meet your happy crying baby is one very unique human experience. And that is how I describe my moments. I can't imagine how my wife would describe each one.

Over the next few sections I am going to tell the birth story of all three of my girls from my perspective. I will demonstrate how my experiences during Labor and Delivery translated to the concepts of this book that can be used by you. I hope by providing you some of these intimate stories, you will not have to experience some of the frustrations and discomforts that come with not being properly prepared for Labor and Delivery in a hospital, as well as not being prepared for an unmedicated vaginal delivery. Like all great heroes in an epic journey, at the beginning I was a mere mortal with only my raw abilities and intuition, but by the 3rd birth I was a Boss-Daddy-Doula with unmatched skills of orated magic and hand to hand contraction combat skills, as well as being totally equipped with an amazing wizards' bag.

Baby E.J.

Daddy Doula Status: Novice Human

Go Bag: Basic Necessities

Pre-Labor Duration: 12-14 hours

Active Labor: 20 hours

Transition Labor: 5 minutes

Thirty-six hours before E.J. was born I was on a golf course with my father-in-law on a hot spring day in Texas. My phone sat in the golf cart console, so I missed the first 12 calls from my wife. At the 16th tee box I checked my phone, and to my dread, the first text message I read was, "I am having contractions. You need to come home now!" The other 10 messages were something along the lines of "Where are you?" Why aren't you answering your phone! CALL ME!!!!!!" So, I yelled at my father in law on the T-box the news that we had to go. Of course, he drilled the par 3 for a hole-in-one! I made it home an hour later to find my wife very upset and scared. Thank goodness the contractions she was having were really light and were spaced around 15 minutes.

There was nothing I could do about the lost time and her fear, I apologized one last time and jumped into my Novus Daddy Doula Mode. I was nervous as hell on the inside, but I felt like my actions were calm. I knew that we were just at the beginning of Pre-labor. What I did not know was how long it was going to be before the contractions were at the 2-minute interval. My wife got on the yoga ball and started bouncing. And like an army private on his first deployment, I started to assemble the Go Bag from zero. Because there was no Daddy Doula Book on the market when EJ was born, my bag was thrown together in a hurry and ended up not being well packed. Below I will break down my first ever Go Bag from the good items I packed, the unnecessary items, and the wish list items.

Good Go Bag Items

- Baby going home outfit

- Birth Plan

- Wife's going home outfit and small makeup bag

- Pillow and blanket for me

- 3 nice athletic shirts

- 1 pair of golf shorts (going home outfit)

- 3 pairs of underwear

- Deodorant

Unnecessary Go Bag items

- Dress shirt – by the end of the stay the shirt was too wrinkled and there was not an iron. I just parted from the hospital with my normal sports shirt with the golf shorts

- Dress shoes for me and my wife – She ended up staying in hospital issued flip flops and I just wore the trainers I was wearing day one.

- Pillow and blanket for my wife - hospital provided adequate bedding for her, but I ended up with some extra bedding.

- Magazines for her – she was either sleeping or nursing so there was not much time for reading.

Wish List Go Bag Items

- Energy drinks

- Personal bedding sheets and padding for the plastic hospital couch

- Soap and shampoo

- Hair product or hat to keep from looking like a wild man.

- Cash –for Vending Machine snacks

- Stainless steel Thermos/Sports bottle

As you can tell I did not pack all the things I really needed for my Go Bag to be successful. But for this moment in time, once it was packed with the essentials for a hospital stay, some of my wife's anxiety eased.

The contractions were regularly spaced at 10 to 15 minutes and held there for hours. Based on our Lamaze class training we knew that we were in Pre-Labor and were hours away before we needed to head to the hospital. Don't let me fool you and portray these hours as a trip to the day spa. We were facing the unknown and our anxiety and stress were high. To help ease some of our stress, we decided to do some contraction meditation and light tickling. The physical attention helped my wife feel secure and comforted, and the action helped me settle into Novice Daddy Doula gradually. We eventually fell asleep around 3:30 P.M. for about 2 hours. Thank goodness we got that brief moment of rest and sleep because it would be 26 hours before we were able to rest again.

My wife awoke from the nap to a massive contraction. Immediately we started measuring the time and interval. After about 4 contraction events, the interval was cut in half in comparison to pre-nap measurements, and the contractions were becoming intense. We also realized this was not going to be a Unicorn L&D so we settled in for the long haul. My wife moved back to the yoga ball to bounce and I cooked us dinner. Looking back, I wish I would have eaten more because breakfast never came. Around 8 o'clock the contractions were at about 5 minutes apart with mild to medium intensity. From my wife's mannerisms I could tell that the contractions definitely hurt, but nothing that would knock her to the ground. The night cooled off, so we hit the streets for some evening walking. Our neighborhood at the time was a one-mile loop. We probably did 3 laps before we decided to go inside for some ball work. After a few hours of bouncing and massaging, the contractions cranked up a few notches. At the time it seemed like

215

these contractions were hard and heavy blows, but with a storyteller's omniscient power, I knew that these contractions were just little jabs preparing her for the big right cross in the 8th round.

Around 11 o'clock P.M. we hit the 2-1-1 contraction interval, but the intensity was still mild. Per our birth plan we decided to go to the L&D hospital's assessment center to make sure that she was in full blown labor. When they hooked her up to the monitors, they quickly realized that she was having Pre-Labor contractions. But when they checked her dilation, she was only at 1 cm. The doctor could not check her into the delivery wing until she was at least measuring 3 cm. After an hour on the monitors and no further progress, they cleared us to go home. But instead of leaving the hospital, the night doctor suggested we do some walking and return in two hours for another check on the dilatation.

Like most hospitals there was a labyrinth of wings to walk. At 1 o'clock A.M. my adrenaline was at zero. I had no cash for the vending machines to get a caffeine rush and there were no stores open in the area. I was a Doula Zombie staggering with my hand on my wife's shoulders rolling the dough with my eyes closed. During our meandering walks through the hospital hallway my wife would stop to go to the bathroom. During these short breaks I would lie down and catch a cat nap. I was a complete wreck, but I don't remember complaining, even though I was in dire need of some kind of an energy jolt. The only thing that kept me going was the pain injected by my wife's hand squeezing my supportive shoulder when a contraction came on.

When we finished the 2 hours walk and returned to the assessment center, the doctor took another look. Thankfully she was at the 3 cm dilatation mark. She was ready to be checked into the labor wing.

It was around 3 A.M. The L&D room was as we expected from our tour of the hospital months prior. There was a long plastic couch that called my name like a Siren to a lost sailor, the TV and computer station, and there was coffee!! I got my wife settled in and while the doctors got her hooked up to the monitors, I snuck out of the room to get some coffee. At the coffee station, there was the normal selection of sugars and creamers for the coffee, but there was also an ice station, tea bags, and chicken broth powder. I made myself a double hazelnut iced latte and chugged it. During this free time, I provided the nursing team a typed Birthing Plan that outlined our goals in bold. I made it clear that we were going to try to go natural with no medications. At no point were the nurses or the doctors to mention epidural unless my wife requested it. Pitocin should only be given if the labor was not progressing and my wife or the baby was in distress. The message was passed along to the night team.

With a new burst of life from my coffee, I moved from zombie mode to just above awake human. At least I was functioning. I set up the hospital TV/computer to our Internet Play List. We were really excited about this feature in the room. We had the option of

Pandora or Netflix streaming through the TV system for the entire labor. What we didn't know was that the sound did not play through the TV speakers, but through the hospital bed phone. The sound was horrible and crackly. It was more annoying than soothing. We decided to turn off the TV system and just play the music through the smart phone. It was better, but not much.

With the music resolved it was time to focus on my wife. The monitor they hooked up to her belly showed the contractions. Basically, the machine worked like this:

1. A base line tension pattern is established.

2. As a contraction starts the line starts to turn upwards. The harder the contraction, the steeper and higher the hill.

3. As the contraction begins to end the line turns down back towards the base line.

I used this monitor to interval my massaging and my words of encouragement. During the valleys I kept it to light massaging or tickling when she was not walking. Note Contraction Meditation had not been invented at this moment in time. Basically, my strategy for this event was as the contraction came on, I would start my words of encouragement. "Here it comes. 2 minutes. You can do this. You are so amazing. Breathe. Look at you. Almost through it. Breath. Try to relax. Okay it is ending. Relax. Relax. You did so great for that one."

The monitor set up the rhythms of my actions. We would use the valleys to either walk or try new positions. In the beginning we just walked. Later we moved to bouncing on the ball. Closer to the end we moved to all fours either slouching on the beds or over the ball. There were a lot of contractions from 2 A.M. to 11 A.M. During the late stages of Active Labor some of the peaks were larger than others. For some of these more intense contractions my Daddy Doula approach was incorrect for the moment. I either did not choose the right words or used the wrong massage technique and was quickly reprimanded. But in the end, I did get some right and was able to keep pushing her through the moment 2 minutes at a time.

Just a quick note on my status; by 5 o'clock A.M. I was starving and coffee was becoming unpalatable, especially for a non-coffee drinker. My wife kept a supply of gum in her purse, so I kept my breath in check. A large cup of chicken broth powder became my snack. But by 9 A.M. I was famished and needed real food. The in-laws showed up to the hospital around 9:30. I was able to get a snickers bar from the vending machine with some money I borrowed from my father in-law while my wife's mom attended her. That would be my only 8-minute break for the L&D. The nurse came and got me out of the waiting room at my wife's request. She needed her Daddy Doula back!

When I returned, her contraction peaks where hitting higher, steeper, and longer. The nursing team transitioned somewhere in between 7 and 8. One of the new nurses checked my wife and she was at 5cm/50%/-3. (5 cm dilated cervix, 50% thinned, and -3 stage in the canal in case you forgot the lingo) The new nurse that checked her knew she had a long way to go based on her measurements and asked her if she wanted to "get total relief", i.e. the epidural. She had not been updated by the nightshift on our Birth Plan. I thought this was going to be the question that broke my wife's will power. She was in pain and wanted relief. She later told me at this moment she thought of her mom and how she brought all of her sisters into the world without an epidural so she knew she could do it. My wife looked at me and I reassured her very firmly that she did not need the epidural now or in the future. During one of the contraction valleys I visited the nurse's station and gave the nurse a stern talking to about our goal and informed her the birth plan is in the file. And we moved on.

Around 9:45. P.M. the doctor came in and said that it would be another 2 hours before transition started. My wife took the news well and I continued to move her through the contractions. Around 10 P.M. we moved into the bathtub. The hot water and the jets really helped her relax. The nurse told her that the tub was not meant for water births so if she hits Transition Labor, she will have to come out. The tub bought us almost two hours of relative relief. We moved her out of the tub and back to the ball. At this point my wife was experiencing the pain of contractions like never before. She was at 7 cm/60%/-1. The contractions were now ascending to their highest peak and her strength was waning. She was exhausted and willpower had broken, or so she thought. We asked the doctor to set up the anesthesiologist for the epidural. Based on a private discussion with the nurse, I knew that it took about 45 minutes of a saline drip to prepare her body for the epidural so that gave my wife a little bit longer. The nurses hooked her up to a saline drip and they also broke her bag of water at the same time. Why the doctor chose not to break them sooner we will never know, but the little intervention and extra time for saline gave her body a window to do some additional work on its own. About an hour later the anesthesiologist showed up. I met him at the door, so my wife did not know that he had arrived. I asked if he could give her 30 more minutes if there was nothing physically wrong with the baby or my wife. He agreed but said that if we don't give her the medicine then, it would probably not take effect in time for her to benefit from the numbing for the transition contractions.

For the next thirty minutes my wife endured the contractions that were lasting over 2 minutes and breaking only for 15 seconds. At the thirty-minute mark the anesthesiologist came in. The nurses where checking her and she was still at 7 cm/60%/-1. For whatever reason, instincts or determination, she decided to push. The nurses told her to stop but she ignored them and locked in like an Olympic Power Lifter and pushed with all her might during the contraction. The contraction meter was off the chart. To the shock of the nurse, my wife pushed the baby down into the birth canal. My wife was now at 9cm/100%/+1. The nurse looked at the anesthesiologist and said "This baby is coming. There will be no need for your services". She then looked at the other nurse and told her, "Get the team together and find the doctor. This baby will be born before lunch!"

The next 5 minutes were something to behold. An 8-person team entered the room. They rolled a cart in that had a lamp on it, hot towels, tools, lubrications. Plastic sheets were spread out; I was put into a cover gown. My wife climbed onto the bed. They asked her what position she wanted to be in. She chose on her back. Two nurses grabbed her right leg and told me to grab her left leg. The doctor arrives and did a quick examination. She looked up at my wife and said "Your baby is ready to come. Are you ready to do this? If so when the next contraction comes on, I want you to push." I really never knew how strong my wife was until she started pushing against me. It took all my might to press her leg back to her chest. It took two nurses to do the same for the right leg.

1st Contraction, 2nd contraction, 3rd, 4th, 5th, 6th ,7th ,8th ,9th,

10th, I could see the baby's head, 11th, I could see her eye brows, 12th I could see her entire head, 13th the doctor grabbed the baby from the canal. The doctor cleared the baby's throat and seemingly tossed her up on my wife's chest. Almost instantly, the sweetest little crackling cry came from our little baby E.J. My wife started to cry, and I started to shake. The room seemed to get small and all I could see was my wife holding E.J. She was this pretty little pink pile of wrinkly love. WOW! Did she have a head of hair! I am not sure how long I was watching her squirm or exactly what was going on around me, but the doctor squeezed my arm and jolted me out of this dream like trance. The doctor handed me a pair of gold scissors that looked a lot like what my mom used for sewing. The doctor placed them in my hand and said "Dad, are you ready to cut your daughters cord?" I nervously inserted my fingers into the eyes of the scissors and the doctor guided me to the cord. I remember feeling the metal glide through E.J.'s cord and hoping that I was not hurting her. The doctor eased the scissors from my fingers and said, "Nice Job Dad".

My wife had done it! She made it through 22 hours of hard natural labor and brought our healthy little girl into the world. Pride, amazement, joy, relief, and love are the describable emotions that were mixing in my heart at that moment. But mostly I was happy. My wife had this glow about her. I think the moment E.J. was in her arms, the last 22 hours vanished, and her heart filled with a new love that only a mother can feel.

Baby K.M.

Daddy Doula Status: Master Doula

Go Bag: Fully loaded with all appurtenances

Pre-Labor Duration: 12-14 hours

Active Labor: 14 hours

Transition Labor: 1 hour 15 minutes

Every time I came to the keyboard to write K.M.'s story, I had the hardest time starting the account of her birth. I basically knew how everything happened, but there just seemed to be little excitement to make a captive story. The end is the best part to this story; mostly because I had a healthy baby in my arms. I know what you are thinking, it was the second pregnancy, so I knew what to expect so it was not as dramatic. That is true. I was also better prepared for the hospital. My Go Bag was packed with all that we needed as described in the Daddy Doula Go Bag two weeks prior to the expected delivery date. I was also not on a golf course when the contractions started. That one choice kept some repeated drama out of K.M.'s story that was good for my Daddy-Doula status.

I guess it is best to start with what was going on with my wife at 36 weeks and 7 days into the pregnancy. She was 7 days past her expected due date (36 weeks is full term of pregnancy). Once she was at 36 weeks, the doctor had my wife going to the assessment center on a daily basis for checkups. Basically, the doctor was monitoring the fluid in the amniotic sack (bag of waters) where the baby lives. The sack is the life support system until the child is born and begins to breathe air. If the water gets to low, the placenta that provides nutrients and oxygen can begin to fail and damage the baby's organs. The experience would be like suffocating slowly. If placenta starts to fail, either the doctor will induce labor with Pitocin or perform an emergency C-section. In K.M.s story, at 5 days the doctor gave us one more day to move things along naturally. In my wife's consultations with the doctor and other mothers we learned of a few "Old Wives Tales" to help with activating labor:

1. Walking
2. Tea
3. Evening Primrose Oil
4. Good ol' hot passionate sex.
5. Spicy food
6. Nipple stimulation

For the last few weeks of the pregnancy she was constantly drinking tea, applying the oils, and walking miles around the neighborhood. Based on our progress the tea and oil were not doing much. We knew that the walking works, but a 9-month pregnant woman can only walk for so long! I was doing my part in participating in mattress Olympics on a regular basis, but still nothing. When my wife got home from the Assessment Center on the day before the deadline we went into "Try It All Mode". We walked, had sex and then loaded the family up in the car and headed to the local Thai Restaurant. My wife ordered the Pad Thai

Noodles Thai Hot. To give you some perspective on her order, most Thai Restaurants offer a range of Mild, Medium, and Hot to satisfy most American consumers. But if you are willing to test your limit and go Thai Hot, you are guaranteed to be sniffling and sweating. The amazing thing about my wife's food order that night was that she is normally a mild heat kind of girl who is sniffling at the aroma of the spice. To jump from Mild to Thai Hot without any warmup meals led to a dinner of tears and statements like "This better work dam it!!" Why would spicy food induce labor contractions? My theory is that the endorphin rush gets the blood pumping, veins contracting and stimulates the body. Whatever the reason, I know one thing; she did not love this form of inducement. My wife was suffering trying to get things moving and I was enjoying the food and the pure entertainment of watching her suffer with every bite. Based on the level of her misery we expected at least a cramp, but no contraction came on. With 5 of 6 Wives Tales tried and no signs of anything happening, we went to the last known option, Nipple Stimulation. When you stop laughing, Sex and Nipple stimulation were actually recommended by the doctor so it must have some merits. You should be excited about this rare opportunity to unlimited access to the nipples. Your partner cannot tell you "No" if it is doctors' orders! After E.J. was down for the night we loaded up a romantic comedy and brought out the Vaseline. For 2 hours I got to "Tune in Tokyo" at 5 minutes on and 5 minutes off. The credits came and still nothing. At that point we decided to head to bed for the night for one more round of the horizontal mambo. We would head to the hospital tomorrow to work out a plan with the doctor about inducing the labor.

To my great shock, something had worked. I think we tuned into Major Tom. At 1 A.M.my wife woke up to a full-on 1-minute contraction. For the next hour the contractions were coming in 5 to 8-minute increments. Around 2 A.M. we decided it was best to get her mother to the house so that we could start doing some laps around the neighborhood. This phase of the labor had an added variable that was not in the first labor, E.J. We had to account for her in all our plans. Thankfully my wife had put her mom on notice earlier in the week to be ready to drop everything to either pick E.J. up to stay with her at her house or to plan on staying at our house. Around 3 A.M. my mother-in-law arrived, I chugged some of my pre-work out powder, and we went to walking. No Zombie walking this time.

Experience makes a difference in every situation. Experience is why there is a balance of rookies and veterans on a football team. Talent can get a rookie running back a few good 100-yard games. Knowing how to rest, recover, and watch film to not miss the blitzing linebacker on a 3rd and 7 in the red zone allows the veteran to get it done game after game for an entire season. For K.M., my wife remembered what the tough contractions felt like. Lap after lap I began to wake up and my wife's contractions got to within 2 minutes. Based on the last delivery experience, my wife knew that the 2 minutes interval was not necessarily an indicator of her progression. She was waiting on the contraction duration to get closer to 1 minute and be a little more severe. We really thought she was close to go-time when the contractions were making my wife vomit. Our neighbor is a fireman. He happened to be getting home around 5 A.M. when he saw my wife chumming the bushes. He shouted from his truck with his typical bright 18 toothed smile, "Good Luck!" After a few miles we decided to go inside to try some relaxation techniques and to rest. After a few hours of relaxing, the contractions slowed from 5 minutes apart to 1 hour apart. We went backwards...

Around 7 A.M. we called the doctor's office and informed them of the change. We asked if we should go to the hospital. The last thing we wanted to do was walk around the cold halls of the hospital for hours before being checked into the delivery room. It took a few hours for the doctor to call back so we both took a quick nap. Around 9 A.M. the doctor called and told us to come in immediately. With the low fluid issue, the doctor felt it was best to get my wife into the delivery room so they could hook her and the baby up to some monitors for close observation. We kissed E.J. goodbye, I grabbed the Go Bag, and we headed out the door. We decided to take a little food detour knowing that my wife would not be able to eat or drink until the baby was born. We crushed some of Georgia's favorite chicken biscuits and made our way to the hospital's assessment center.

Seemingly as soon as we arrived, the nurse hooked my wife up to the contraction monitor and added a second monitor that was specifically used to monitor the baby's heartrate. After a quick check my wife was at 2cm/50%/-3 dilation, but contractions were still an hour apart. At this stage, the hospital would normally turn us away, but because of the low fluid and the danger to the baby, they checked us into our room.

We were checked in the room around 11 A.M. A few minutes later the nurse had my wife set up with an IV connection for fluids and the potential administration of Pitocin. I began unpacking the Go Bag. The first thing I did was set up the music and then I began passing out the Birthing Plan to all the nurses. I highlighted to the nurses that even though there were some risks to the baby because of the low fluid, our goal was still to go as natural as possible and to stick to our plan where we could. The doctor evaluated my wife one more time and reported no progress. Based on the risks to the baby and the lack of progress, the doctor informed us that we had 3 hours to get contractions going and more dilatation or she was going to intervene and medically induce the labor with Pitocin. If the heart rate dropped below 80 bpm and remained there after a contraction at any time during the 3-hour period, the doctor was going to order the C-Section.

Based on our new deadline, at this point we had two options:

1. Wait for her body to do all the work, but risk no progress and have to use Pitocin, or
2. Start manual manipulation of the cervix.

In either case, the baby was being monitored closely. We decided to roll the dice and not go with an epidural. No epidural would allow my wife to be awake in the event the C-Section was ordered. If a C-section was the doctor's call to ensure the safety of the baby, my wife would be given anesthesia for the surgery. With all options weighed, we asked the nurse to break the bag of waters. After the quick procedure, I convinced my wife to let me get lunch in the hospital cafeteria. It would give me a slight break (30 minutes) and the food would give me the energy to make the final leg as her Daddy Doula.

I arrived back to the L&D room around 1:15 P.M. Seemingly within 15 minutes of me getting back to the room, my wife was in full-on contractions. 1 minute long and 2 minutes apart. For a few hours we went through the cycles of the contractions. Massaging, words of encouragement, and slow dancing were in full implementation. When the monitor was peaking like Mount Denali, we headed for the bathtub. For some reason the bath provided little relief to her. My wife lasted about 30 minutes in the tub before we were back to the ball for leg massaging with some Quadra-Vice being applied intermittently. Over the course of the last few hours, there had been a few moments the monitor showed the baby's heart rate around 80 during the contraction. The nurses watched intently, but every time the baby recovered quickly after the contraction. Around 5 o'clock that evening, the doctor came in to do an assessment of my wife's progress. There was no measurement reported just a quick statement, "Are you ready to deliver your baby?" My wife was a little befuddled by the sudden proclamation of being on the home stretch and was simultaneously excited about pushing. In her mind because of her experience with the birth of EJ, she was only 12 pushes away from meeting her new baby girl.

After about 30 minutes and 20 good strong pushes, the baby was not coming even though my wife was pushing with all her might. It turns out the baby was sunny-side-up and caught on the pelvic bone. When the baby is facing down the neck can bend and roll past the pelvic bone. When the baby is facing up the baby can only bend its head back so far. In a head up position the contraction pushes the baby down, but the chin gets caught on the pelvic bone stopping the downward movement. Not only did the bone make it hard to push the baby out of the already tiny opening, it apparently hurt like hell.

During the first 45 minutes of transition labor I had been holding one of my wife's powerful legs, pressing it to her chest for each contraction. She had me by the shoulders to help her basically gain grip to do a Power Man 5000 crunch. On about the 30th contraction and pushing attempt, I was tiring, and my wife was becoming exhausted. The only thing she had to keep her going was the idea of meeting her new baby and the adrenaline from the pain. The good news was that the baby's heart rate was strong on the monitor so no medical intervention was required as long as my wife could keep pushing. The doctor decided to apply some lubricating gel to her fingers and wedged them between the pelvic bone and the baby's jaw. The doctor told my wife on the next contraction to give it everything, and for me and the nurses to push her legs back as far we could. She was basically going to shoehorn the head out. When the contraction came on, my wife pushed, and I pressed. It was like bench pressing 300lbs because of the amount of force she was pushing back against me. At about 15 seconds into the contraction the baby slid down and hit the pelvic bone. In her extreme exertion of power, my wife's arm slipped around my neck. She had me in a WWF headlock that not even the Macho Man could have escaped. Looking back, I was lucky her forearm was on the back of my neck and was not a few more inches over the artery. It would have been a 5 second KO by Guillotine. Fortunately for me, the baby's head hit the slippery fingers of the doctor and popped out from behind the pelvic bone. With a little more effort by my wife and the doctor, the baby slipped right into the doctor's hands. The doctor immediately places the baby on my wife's chest, and we heard for the first time K.M sound out her happy cry. Mom and daughter were united. It took me about a minute to recover from my wife's headlock. But when I did, all I could feel was joy and love. When I was cutting the cord, I was not as nervous as I was with EJ. Even though this was my second Daddy Doula experience, I was just as mesmerized as the first time. I never would have guessed that my heart could grow even bigger.

Baby J.J.

Daddy Doula Status: Boss Doula

Go Bag: Fully loaded with all appurtenances

Pre-Labor Duration: 2 hours

Active Labor: 1 hour and 20 minutes

Transition Labor: 5 minutes

Yes, we went for the boy! No, it was a girl. And yes, I am equally thrilled that I have another daughter. They say girls come home to take care of their daddy. Boys leave and only come home for their mommy. I will leave it at that. And don't let the metrics above fool you. This was no short and easy Labor and Delivery journey. The heavy action was short relative to the other childbirths, but the time to get there was grueling.

Back to JJ. To keep the third pregnancy fresh and even more special, we made the gender a surprise! The gender would not be revealed to us until I looked at the baby to cut the umbilical cord. I remember when the moment came; my heart was already racing from the delivery, but the added anticipation brought a new sense of being human to the moment. Other than having to snip twice at the cord, not much was different to what I did to help my wife get through the knee buckling pain of childbirth. If we have seemingly covered most of the action of labor and delivery, what remains to help you get through your D-Day moment that we have not covered in depth with E.J. and K.M.? I believe some finer details that emerged because of how the labor progressed will complete the required education to be a Daddy Doula.

Before we get into the Labor and Delivery, let me recap a few things that stand out about this pregnancy that were completely different than with the other girls:

1. Time Management: Unlike with the previous two pregnancies, my wife and I did not have a lot of down time to practice relaxation techniques or to attend a refresher Lamaze class. The two girls consumed a lot of our spare time and energy. When you have two under 2, there are a ton of diapers to change, strong wills to guide, and sprouting spirits to nurture. I failed here and wish I could have made the effort to carve out more time for the two of us to connect more to the pregnancy. It comes down to choices and I made a few selfish ones during this period.

2. General Pregnancy Connectivity: For this pregnancy, I felt like I was as connected as a 1990s cell phone in South Georgia. My job seemingly was keeping me from all the baby appointments. The girls were demanding all my energy when I got home. My wife, being the super woman that she is, just carried on with no complaints> I believe she understood that my career was evolving and was at critical point for future growth, so she did not burden me with additional commitments. We were both so busy it felt like it was all we

could do to make time for a date night here and there just so our marriage could stay connected.

3. Nursery Planning: Because we did not know the gender of the baby, we did not update the nursery design. Instead we created a special room for K.M. She seems to really love panda's, so my wife created a cool black and white room that was complimented by a large stuffed panda bear we named Echo. We painted the room ourselves and had someone else handle the refurbishing of the furniture. My wife added her custom art to bring the colors and the panda theme of the room together. Since the third child was a sweet little girl, the nursery was good-to-go with its lanterns and coral cuteness. No updates required for a few years, or until J.J. realizes she gets an opinion.

4. L&D Preparedness: Let's just put it this way, we were Mrs. Sexy Prego and Daddy Doula. Straight up professional birthing bad asses. The Go Bag was legendary; compact and complete with the perfect assortments of comfort, food, and doula tools. Our Birth Plan was kept crisp in a vanilla binder and passed out to the nursing staff like briefs in a Law and Order episode. We understood that even with the lack of practice, we were confident in ourselves, our history, and our connection to do it one more time *all-nat-ur-al.*

Now that you have a little insight into where we were at regarding our connection, let me let you in on some additional 3rd child pregnancy reality; it was not as sweet, romantic, and novel as the previous pregnancies. Life as parents changed how we were able to prepare and connect to the pregnancy. In hindsight, I believe being parents, more so a parenting team, kept the pregnancy connection smoldering in our hearts. When D-Day finally came the moment seized us. It only took a couple of laps around the neighborhood to add the required oxygen to the pregnancy connection to rekindle the fire. My point here is that our previous two pregnancies and labor experiences had prepared us for the upcoming 24-hour journey to bring J.J. into the world. There are no short cuts to being ready to be a Daddy Doula. If this is your first or your third pregnancy, you must have her trust to be successful in natural birth. I feel this is a truth because in the 18 months between birthdays, I never lost that connection and I was the Boss-Daddy Doula helping my wife achieve her unmedicated goal.

I hope some of the finer details of the childbirth of J.J will provide you with additional insight into what it is like on D-Day. As I stated previously, there was not a lot of time for preparing for the pregnancy. But around 36 weeks, my wife and I set aside an hour to generate the birth plan. Our first priority was still to go un-medicated for the birth. We changed up a couple of post-delivery actions like the eye-salve application and the vitamin K shot. (See Birth Plan – Post Delivery for additional information on these decisions.) We also decided that she was going to deliver on all fours instead of on her back. You might recall from the first two births that when my wife was on her back during transition. She had to use all her strength to push while the nurses and I were doing a fair amount of work pushing her legs back in the opposite direction to maximize the contraction. To try to make the pushing phase a little easier, we were going to let gravity assist the contraction. When the laboring woman is on all fours, standing, or squatting the birth canal stays wide open. Whereas when she is on her back, the abdomen typically compresses and rolls the pelvic up, which makes the opening smaller. Again, I would remind you not to force any position and let her instincts tell her what is best for the moment.

In our discussion that night we also did decide to approach the contractions and breaks slightly different. When I was using my "Words of Affirmation" I would no longer refer to the contraction as a contraction, but instead refer to it as a wave. Our mind set was that waves come and go. During the storm of labor, we knew that the waves will also vary in frequency and amplitude. But no matter how fierce, the wave would pass by at some point and leave calmer waters behind the crash. For instance, I would say, "Okay baby, here comes a wave." Or "You are being so brave and strong. The wave is almost over." Like with the other L&Ds, I would use the contraction monitor to predict the wave and remind her of its temporary fury and future relief. Generally, her mind set for the labor was going to be not to fight the contraction, but to just let it hit, accept it, and let it go through its cycle. Looking back now at the labor process of JJ, the acceptance mind set allowed her to relax more during and after the contraction event. With the wave mind set we were able to attempt the Contraction Meditation techniques during the breaks of Pre-Labor and Active Labor. I have no empirical evidence to prove that Contraction Meditation worked, but she was more relaxed during the rest period of the contractions which might have had the positive effect desired because she transitioned quickly from Active labor to transition labor. As the contractions grew longer, more powerful and she had shorter rests, it became impossible to keep up the meditation practices.

At the 35-week appointment, my wife was 1/50%/-10. The amniotic fluids s looked good and the baby was healthy and strong. There had been no real contractions other than a stomach virus for a few days. The false contractions forced a call to the Grandparents and put them into the impending L&D reality. Even though it was a false alarm, Neenie and Paki had their Go Bags ready for the real midnight call.

At the 36-week appointment (Full Term), my wife was 2/50%/-10. Fluids were good and the Baby was healthy and strong. (To help with the chronology of the story, the appointment was on a Wednesday) Also this was my first appointment to see the little alien in an ultrasound. During the appointment the doctor informed us that the 37-week mark was the limit because this was our third baby. Apparently the longer the term for the 3rd child there is a risk of the baby being a still-born because the placenta failure is greater. With the doctor's advice, we booked a Sunday appointment for a scheduled induction so that our primary doctor could deliver the baby on Monday. She was off that weekend and we would be delegated the backup Doc. With the induction on the hospital schedule, before we left the hospital the doctor agreed to the following birth plan and entered it into the hospital notes:

1. Birth Plan: No intervention unless doctor informed us that the baby is in danger.
2. Plan of Action in the event intervention is required:

> Option 1: Break Bag of Waters to kick start labor. Wait for contractions to start. (4- 6 Hours) If not working move to Option 2
> Option 2: Administer Pitocin. Duration is until the baby is born, baby or mother is in danger, or contractions are not increasing the dilatation, effacement, and position.

> Option 3: Immediate C- Section if baby is in danger.

It was very important that the doctor recorded our plan into the medical notes since she was not going to be working that weekend Another doctor in the practice was working that weekend. In the event of a delivery on Friday, Saturday, or Sunday night, my wife's primary doctor would not be available. The doctor did say that if the timing was right, she would cut into her weekend activities to deliver our final baby into the world. (One of the reasons we chose her practice because she was dedicated to her patients) The doctor's commitment to being available for a set window set into motion a series of decisions that affected the birth plan.

On the Friday after settling the Sunday induction appointment, I woke up at my usual 4:30 A.M. for my morning 3-mile run. A good run in the morning before work always clears my head and makes for a productive day. Plus, there was really no harm since nothing was happening until Sunday... What was I thinking!?!?!?

That morning, after I had left for work, my wife went to the restroom and found brown mucus mixed with a bloody discharge when she wiped. This Brown/Blood discharge is called "Show" and is normal while having contractions or at the onset of Active labor. To my wife this was really no issue because she was not having contractions. Around 4 p.m. she discovers another batch of the discharge. My wife is having a normal day with no contractions and starts to get concerned because of the "still born" risks.

At 5 P.M. we call the doctor's office to ask about the color of discharge and go on a walk

At 6 P.M. the on-call doctor advises us to go straight to the L&D wing - Still no contractions.

At 7:30 P.M. Neenie arrives to take the girls to her house. We inform her that we are going to the Assessment Center only. If the baby is healthy, we are coming home.

At 9 P.M. we arrived at the assessment center. Once we are in, they locked us down. Turns out the doctor had put in her notes that if there is any progress or issues, my wife was to be admitted.

Results of Assessment: Baby is healthy and strong but there was a "variable" in the heart rate. (Variable = Heart Rate went from 125 bpm to 80 bpm for a few seconds). Now we must check in to monitor the baby because my wife was over 37 weeks.

Like with every natural birth, you can only plan. When you are in the moment, all you can do is hope you are nimble and knowledgeable enough to adapt to what life throws at your well thought out plan.

Good News 1: The on-call doctor, residents, and nurses were well aware of our birth plan. Not only did each have the hard copy I passed out, they had the notes from Wednesday meeting.

Good News 2: The medical team was going to try to ensure the delivery of the baby sometime Saturday afternoon during the primary doctor's window. That choice meant that even though we were checked in, no intervention would happen until the morning, unless the baby became distressed during the night.

Good News 3: We got to sleep!!! Some. If I had to go 30 to 48 hours on 6 hours of sleep, I had enough of my pre-workout powder in my Go Bag to sustain me through two sunrises, all being it I would be shaking like Miley Cyrus.

Remember in *Chapter 5.2 Picking Your OBGYN* and *in Chapter 5.4 Creating Your Birth Plan* I discussed making sure your doctors and the staff is supportive of your plan. Well this medical team was exemplary of a doctor-patient trust by supporting our birth plan. The doctors and residents reviewed our plan and explained their concerns about the situation. In the end, health limits and durations were agreed upon. The medical team, my wife and I knew exactly when each labor intervention option would be exhausted. The plan became a little more detailed than Wednesday's plan The Birth Plan was revised as follows:

1.   The baby's heart rate is monitored throughout the night. As long as a heart distress incident is not detected in the baby, no intervention is required. (Sustained decline or long intervals below 80 BPM requires intervention). Mom and Dad are allowed to sleep. Unleash the Go Bag.

2.   Walking and ball work will be performed throughout the night to expedite progress. These two activities were performed between 11P.M. to 2 A.M. and 6A.M. to 10 A.M. at different intervals to keep our legs fresh. A. small caveat to the birth plan was that at 2 A.M. Saturday my wife had to show dilation progress, or the bag of waters would be broken which could speed up the process. If this happened the primary doctor would not be able to deliver the baby.

If progress at 2 A.M. but still no contractions at 10 A.M. the bag of waters will be broken. Four hours will be allotted for Active Labor to begin.

If active labor has not begun by 2 P.M. Saturday Pitocin will be administered. The Pitocin plan was as follows:

1.   2 mg/Liter every 20 minutes until contractions start or are on a regular contraction interval. Maximum dosage is 36

mg/liter.

2. Pitocin will be administered no longer than 6 hours or less if the baby becomes distressed.

3. C-Section. General Anesthesia. Daddy Doula does skin to skin. Breast feeding might be harder because of the anesthesia and dad has to possibly give formula until mother recovers. 3 days in hospital and 2 to 4 weeks of home care.

At around 1:00 A.M. Saturday morning there were still no contractions. We were just walking around the 14th floor passing the same nurses and doctors like we were at a "Wear your scrubs night" at the roller-skating ring. Note: 15 laps = 1 mile according to my person step counter. At 3 miles we went in for the 2 A.M. assessment. The resident measured 3cm/60%/-3. Yeah! PROGRESS!! The bag of waters did not have to be broken and we were still on plan for Saturday delivery. The resident doctor and my wife agreed to stretch her to 4cm and strip the membrane one last time to see if Active Labor would initiate on its own. After the membrane was stripped it was time to rest until the morning. I think it took me about 5 seconds to fall asleep once the yoga mat and sheets were in place.

At 7 A.M. Saturday morning we went back to walking. I ordered in breakfast. We shared the food and she chugged water even though she really was not supposed to in the event anesthesia was required. We hit our daily 10,000-step goal at 9 A.M. Before we knew it, 10 A.M. was staring our birth plan down. The on-call doctor came into to assess the situation – 4cm/60%/-3. No change since 2 A.M. It was time to break the bag of waters. We had 6 hours to get things going without medical intervention.

At 3 P.M., nothing was happening. Small talk was getting old and the view of the medical center was getting stale. The nurse came in for a friendly reminder that the on-call doctor has given her one additional hour before further intervention. The nurse also informed us that there was a chance the primary doctor's window for the Saturday delivery would be missed. Based on the new information, my wife chose to have the first round of Pitocin right then. She was frustrated all around because she really wanted to avoid any medical intervention. Pitocin is considered a medical intervention, but it only affects the mother's body. Pitocin is a synthetic hormone that tricks the woman's body to start contracting. All the other body functions just react, so I would consider it as close to a natural birth as you can get as long as pain medication is not used during the labor. At this point, pride and a "natural" birth do not matter to us because it is about safety of the baby. With that mind set, my wife's frustration was shortly overcome by her eagerness to meet her little baby.

I am about to go through the sequence of the Pitocin and try to give you some insights of what to expect once administered. Pitocin's goal is to kick start contractions and keep them at regular intervals. The intensity is directly related to the milligrams added.

At each level of Pitocin, the interval and the intensity will be the same. No Breaks or lighter contractions! Regular like TBS channel's reruns of "Friends". To my wife's credit, she is still determined to have a non-medicated vaginal delivery even though this was the moment to ask for an epidural.

For the remainder of the story, keep in mind that I am using the contraction monitor as my point of reference to determine when contractions happen. I am using my wife's Zina Warrior Yell as my gage to the labor stage: active or transition labor. The Pitocin is added in 2 mg intervals. The level is only increased if the contraction cycle does not stay regular (2-1-1) or speed up (1-2-1), or if dilation is not progressing (4cm to 5 cm).

Round 1. 2mg – 20 minutes: Small contractions begin. Contractions are between 5-0.5-2 and 2-1-1. My wife no longer wants to walk. She only wants ball work. Monitor is reading little humps, or small contraction strength. We are trying the contraction meditation practices in conjunction with the wave philosophy.

Shoulder Doe massages and Spider Fingers for goose bumps, Words of encouragement during the contraction, and general relaxation practice after the contraction event

Round 2. 4mg – 60 minutes: Distinct peaks being observed on the monitor. Contractions are 1-1-1. I placed a chair in front her while she sets on top of the ball to give her something to grip onto for stability.

Sweeping the leg, Spider Fingers, Words of encouragement. Referencing the waves and not fighting the moment. Relaxation Practice on many of the contraction events, but towards the end it was impossible.
Zina Warrior Yell - just getting fired up

Round 3. 8mg– 60 minutes. My wife foregoes the 6 mg interval because she is handling the pain and is ready for it to be over. Contractions are 1-2-1. Wide Peaks being observed on the monitor. Contractions are lasting longer than the breaks.

Sweeping the leg, Spider Fingers, and Shoulder Dough. Words of encouragement. Referencing the waves.
Zina Warrior Yell – Full active labor. At one point she hit a perfect C-Note. I literally laughed out loud when I thought she was singing "Let it Go"

The pain is real now. Requests for the epidural are frequent. *Daddy Doula fully engaged!!* There is no turning back now. Epidural will do nothing. Pain Medication could be provided, but it is not even suggested.

Round 4. 10mg– 20 minutes. Labor is on like Donkey Kong!

My wife adamantly requests to be checked. 6cm/90%/0.

Nurse tells my wife she is progressing and asks if she feels like she needs to push. She responds, "I think I have to Poo". Nurse says to wait 15 minutes so that she can get the bed pan ready. My wife thinks she is talking about getting a chamber pot to poop in...

Nurse starts making the calls. The birth cart is prepped. Gauze strips counted. Baby Warmer turned on.

The wave analogy is hard to relate too and keep using, but my words are conveying power, resilience, and calmness

Quadra-Vice deployed in 1-2-1 intervals. My pecks and triceps are fully engaged and burning.

Round 5. 0 mg – Nurse turns the Pitocin off. The Primary Doctor is leaving her date at the restaurant. On-Call doctor is sprinting through the hospital maze to the room. (Note If the body is doing the work, no need for Pitocin)

My wife climbs into the bed, without instruction, and readies herself in the position on all fours. (Birth Plan taking over)

On-Call Doctor shows up and assesses. Baby is ready to come on the next contraction. 10cm/100%/+1. Primary Doctor shows up at the labor room door. The two doctors meet in the middle of the room like a WWE tag team with a high five at the bed ropes to bring in the Pin Doctor. Funny side note, the primary doctor has her "Going Out Top" on, a pair of nice jeans to match, with wedge shoes. She calmly instructs my wife to start pushing as she pulls on her blue cover and face shield. My wife smiles because she hears the familiar sweet voice of her doctor commanding the room.

Two pushes. My wife instinctually rolls over to her side. Doctor slides a foot pad into place for her to push against. My job is to push the other leg. Side Power Man 5000 Crunches! The Contraction monitor is peaking. 1 push – 2 push – 3 push, I can see the head. 4 – 5. Welcome to the world our sweet baby... Oh shit! Why are you blue? Why are you not crying?

Doctor grabs a suction thing-a-ma-gig and inserts into throat. 1 second – 2 seconds – I hear a little whimper and a happy crying baby is placed on mom's chest.

Clapping, words of elations and big smiles fill the room.

What is it? What is it? Is the chant in the room? The doctor hands me the scissors and opens the legs to give access to the cord. In a long second, I gasp and whisper, "It is a girl. J.J.". Snip and Snip. We Did It!!.....Holy Shit!! Exhale....

Remember this one factoid about induced labor by Pitocin. It can be the NOX to a Fast and Furious L&D. There was a small window at about 8mg of Pitocin that we could have supplied the epidural numbing juice. In that window, it will take a courageous woman and a Boss Daddy Doula to keep the Epidural out of the room when the contractions are on full tilt. After seeing the pain my wife went through, I cannot imagine any woman getting past 12 mg/liter of Pitocin without asking for the epidural. If more Pitocin is what it takes to keep the contractions going and she still wants to have a vaginal delivery without an epidural, your partner's will power and resilience will be indescribable. You should bow to her in worship every day after your child is born.

Chapter 11:
3 Days and Home

At the end of the childbirth journey, I really hope that you are the proud father of a healthy crying baby. You should be very proud of your partner no matter the path that unfolded. You should even give yourself a little pat on the back for being the loving and supportive Daddy Doula you always had in you.

Now that the dramatic part of labor and delivery is over, you are probably a little curious about the length of time you will spend in the hospital after this great life event. You might also be wondering how you will spend that time in the Post Delivery Room. Generally, how much laboring you do at the house will determine the total time you spend in the hospital, because post birth is generally under contract by insurance and the hospital. The general rule for the length of your hospital stay is as follows:

1. Vaginal Birth = 2 nights from the time of the birth.
2. C-Section = 3 nights from the time of the operation.

If there are complications, then you could be stuck there for a week or longer looking after your partner and baby.

Now that you have your mind wrapped around the time you should expect to be in the hospital, let's get you ready for the post delivery.

No matter what time of day or night that your little booboo, stud muffin, princess, or love-joy comes into the world, you and your partner are going to be exhausted. The adrenalin of the moment that has carried you both for the last 24 hours will fade, and you will both be reaching for the light switch and pillow. The only problem is that you now have a baby that needs to feed every 2 hours and will have a diaper to be changed every hour. The nurses and doctors will be in and out of the room checking the mom and baby; drawing blood, foot printing, and having you fill out paperwork. So, in short, your L&D Daddy Doula duties are over, but your post-partum Daddy Doula duties have just begun.

Your role in Post-Partum is to remain supportive, encouraging, and attentive. For you the primary action is over, but your partner's body will still be working. Her body must learn how to cope to the sudden change of environment. She is no longer a host. Her body will also have to gear up for milk production and the core of her brain functions have to adapt to help her become an empathetic mother. All these post-partum changes are triggered by hormones. According to Mayo Clinic, the mother is the most susceptible to experiencing mood swings, crying spells, anxiety, and difficulty sleeping with in the first 3 days after delivery. These emotional states during the first few days are described as the "post-partum baby blues." But some moms will experience long term and more severe depression that is identified as "post-partum depression". Most of the issues are due to dramatic drops in estrogen and progesterone, as well as other hormones produced by the thyroid that are physically affecting how her body feels. But there are other emotional issues like identity, body awareness, and loss of control that can be adding to her blues.

To help you as a post-Partum Daddy – Doula, I want to provide following general symptoms for Post-Partum Blues and Post-Partum Depression, as well as the associated risk factors courtesy of the Mayo Clinic:

Post-Partum Blues

1. Mood swings
2. Anxiety
3. Sadness
4. Irritability
5. Feeling overwhelmed
6. Crying
7. Reduced concentration
8. Appetite problems
9. Trouble sleeping

Post-Partum Depression

1. Depressed mood or severe mood swings
2. Excessive crying
3. Difficulty bonding with the baby
4. Withdrawing from family and friends
5. Loss of appetite or eating much more than usual
6. Inability to sleep (insomnia) or sleeping too much
7. Overwhelming fatigue or loss of energy

8. Reduced interest and pleasure in activities once enjoyed

9. Intense irritability and anger

10. Fear of not being a good mother

11. Feelings of worthlessness, shame, guilt or inadequacy

12. Diminished ability to think clearly, concentrate or make decisions

13. Severe anxiety and panic attacks

14. Thoughts of harming yourself or your baby

15. Recurrent thoughts of death or suicide

Risk factors

Postpartum depression can develop after the birth of any child, not just the first. Depression can occur at any time up to two years after the birth. The risk increases if you:

1. have a history of depression, either during pregnancy or at other times

2. have bipolar disorder

3. had postpartum depression after a previous pregnancy

4. have family members who've had depression or other mood stability problems

5. have experienced stressful events during the past year, such as pregnancy complications, illness or job loss

6. the baby has health problems or other special needs

7. have difficulty breast-feeding

8. have problems in your relationship with your spouse or significant other

9. have financial problems

10. had a pregnancy that was unplanned or unwanted

Post-Partum Blues can last days, weeks, and even months after the delivery. The symptoms can even arise if a C-section was performed.

Post-Partum Blues and depression should not be taken lightly. The effects on the mother can be destructive and dangerous to both her and the baby. Please consult your doctor to discuss further how to identify, cope, and treat Post-Partum Blues and Depression. Most mothers who are experiencing the blues or depression will not be aware of their condition. It will be up to you as the Daddy Doula to be aware of her changes and proactive if you start noticing these conditions arise.

Now that you are on alert, let's focus on the two to three days you will spend in the hospital. On par with the overall theme of sleep during L&D, there is still little sleep to be had post-delivery; but you will have lots of free time. I suggest the following activities to help you stay connected to the new Mom and possibly ease her mind:

1. Change all the diapers so that you will be an expert by the time you leave.

2. Perfect the towel swaddle (Even though you have brought the engineered swaddles in your Go Bag).

3. Massage your baby's Mom a few times a day with the nice oil you bought.

4. Give her a hot lavender sponge bath each day.

5. Watch her favorite shows and movies with her.

There are three reasons why you should perform the suggested activities listed.

Reason 1: Any effort you make to remove activities from her plate will allow her to recover more quickly.

Reason 2: Your acts of service and physical touch will keep the connection between the two of you going and provide her reassurance of your commitment.

Reason 3: Once you leave the hospital, she will lose all her nursing support. The two of you will be on your own having to deal with the challenges of your new life. Think of the days after the delivery in the hospital as if you were going to a little baby resort. It is the only time you will have 24-hour support for tending to all the needs of the baby and the mother. Once you get home, it is either you or your mother-n-law that will be the support. If your partner had to have a C-section, she will be on bed rest and unable to lift anything over 15 pounds for weeks. So, if you had a mountain sized baby, you will be handling the baby from the crib to the breast, breast to the changing table, and back to the crib. Take my advice and try to relax as much as you can while you are at the hospital. Especially help your partner relax as much as she can. It will be the last chance you get to relax until the baby is sleeping through the night.

Chapter 12:
Go forth and Become the Daddy Doula

Somewhere in the time between me finding out that I was going to be a father and becoming the father of three girls, I realized that men can choose to be in different role during the pregnancy and childbirth other than the traditional hands-off model portrayed in pop culture. I learned that the father no longer must set idle while the mother literally and figuratively grows with the baby. The father can participate in the developments of the pregnancy and be an active force in the delivery experience of the mother. As you know from reading this book that it is was not easy for me to change my mind set and want to be in the same emotional space as my wife in regard to the pregnancy. It was a long mental game. I had to keep forcing myself away from a TV full of March Madness and Fantasy Football to make time to help my wife with her little projects, get to understand how her body was changing, and to prepare for the trials of the delivery. The labor was especially taxing on my patience and mental fortitude. It is no easy task to be sweet, encouraging, strong, and thick-skinned for over 24 hours on 2 hours of sleep. I know it sounds like I am grumbling about how much I sacrificed. I am human and I resisted the change. But like all great challenges and tribulations of life, if you survive you will come out the other end changed. All the little moments of each pregnancy are etched in my heart and have made me appreciate my wife and my experience with her more deeply. It has been easy to tell these stories because each has become part of my story. I really hope that I have inspired you to take on the same challenge.

During this season of my life I have come to know a few truths about life. Each became crystal clear after I helped bring my little love-joys into the world:

1. My wife is more powerful and courageous than either she or I knew. She is capable of anything that she puts her heart and mind into.

2. My wife and I are one hell of a team. We can get through anything that life or marriage throws at us if we approach the situation with the same fervor as childbirth.

3. There is no better feeling than holding your child for the first time while your partner gives you that look of gratitude for being a part of helping her bring life into the world.

Good Luck Gentlemen! And give yourself a pat on the back and a man-card reward for reading this book. I hope that it has provided a few tools that will help alleviate some of your anxiety around the pregnancy and childbirth. With a head full of knowledge, I hope that you now have the ability to go through this brief moment in your life fully present and with your heart wide open.

APPENDIX A:
Daddy Doula Workouts

CARDIO STARTER

Warm Up: 6 Minutes (30 Seconds each exercise)

1. Jog/Butt Kicks
2. High Knees
3. Jumping Jacks
4. Side to Side Floor Touches

Stretching: 4 minutes (30 Seconds each exercise)

1. Hamstring Stretch - Left/Right
2. Groin Stretch – Left/Right
3. Calves – Left/Right
4. Quad Stretch– Left Right
5. Front Dive/Back Dive
6. Scissor Arms

Work Out: 10 Minutes

1. Run-Walk: 4 Minutes (30 sec run-30 secs walk)
2. Push Ups: 1-minute Max Reps (minimum 10 reps)
3. Run-Walk: 4 Minutes (30 secs run-30 secs walk)
4. Push Ups: 1-minute Max Reps (minimum 10 reps)

Cool Down: 2 minutes (30 seconds each exercise)

1. Hamstring Left/Right

2. Groin Lunge Left Right

3. Calves

4. Quads

CARDIO POWER

Warm Up: 6 Minutes

1. Jog/Butt Kicks
2. High Knees
3. Jumping Jacks
4. Side to Side Floor Touches

Stretching: 4 minutes

1. Hamstring Stretch - Left/Right
2. Groin Stretch - Left Right
3. Calves
4. Quads
5. Front Dive/Back Dive
6. Scissor Arms

Cardio Power: 32 Minutes

Round 1 (x 3) = 6 minutes

1. Jump Rope – 30 sec
2. Power Jacks– 30 sec
3. Suicide Sprints (5 Yards)– 30 sec
4. Jump Knees– 30 sec

1-minute Break for Water and Journal entry

Round 2 (x2) = 8 minutes

1. Power Knees Left – 1 min

2. Fast feet to Jump Turns – 1 min

3. Power Knees Right - 1 min

4. Fast feet to Jump Turns – 1 min

1-minute Break for Water and Journal entry

Round 3 (x3) =6 minutes

1. Front Kick Right– 30 sec

2. Pogo Left Leg– 30 sec

3. Front Kick Left– 30 sec

4. Pogo Right – 30 sec

1-minute Break for Water and Journal entry

Round 4 = 10 minutes

1. Basketball Shots Right – 1 minute

2. Side Plank Center/Left/Center/Right/Center – 1 minute

3. Basketball Shots Left – 1 minute

4. Mountain Climbers – 1 minute

5. Side Jacks– 1 minute

6. Fast feet Burpees (10 Count)

7. Speed Jacks – 1 minute

8. Power Push Ups– 1 minute

9. Low Squat Jabs– 1 minute

10. Speed Bag– 1 minute

Cool Down: (2 Minutes)

1. Deep Breaths – 30 seconds

2. Hamstring Stretch – 30 seconds each leg

3. Groin Stretch – 30 seconds each leg

4. Quad Stretch – 30 seconds each leg

POWERHOUSE

Warm Up: 6 Minutes

1. Jog/Butt Kicks
2. High Knees
3. Jumping Jacks
4. Side to Side

Stretching: 4 Minutes

1. Hamstring Left/Right
2. Groin Lunge/twist Left Right
3. Calves
4. Quads
5. Front Dive/Back Dive
6. Scissor Arms

Power Mix: 35 Minutes

Strength Round 1 = 10 minutes

1. Push Up Jacks – 10 Reps
2. Back Flies – 10 Reps
3. Shoulder Press – 10 Reps
4. Curls – 10 reps
5. Crunchy Frogs or Toe Touches – 10 Reps

1-minute Break for Water and Journal entry

Cardio Round 2 (x3) = 6 Minutes

1. Jump Rope – 30 sec
2. Box Jump– 30 sec
3. Suicide Sprints– 30 sec
4. Side Jacks– 30 sec

1-minute Break for Water and Journal entry

Cardio Round 2 (x3) = 6 Minutes

1. Power Knees Left – 30 sec
2. Long Jumps 30 sec
3. Power Knees Right 30 sec
4. Ice Skaters - 30 sec
5. 1-minute Break for Water and Journal entry
6. Power Round 3 (x3) = 2 Minutes
7. Step Back Lunge to Jump Right – 30 sec
8. Step Back Lunge to Jump Left – 30 sec

Bonus = 10 Minutes

1. Basketball Shots Right – 1 minute
2. Basketball Shots Left – 1 minute
3. Fast feet Burpees - 2 minutes
4. Push Ups – 1 minute
5. Horse Squat Jabs– 1 minute
6. Speed Bag– 1 minute

Cool Down 5 Minutes:

1. Deep Breaths
2. Hamstring Left/Right

3. Groin Lunge/twist Left Right

4. Calves

5. Quads

6. Front Dive/Back Dive

7. Scissor Arms

http://www.mom365.com/wisdom/moms/birth%20survey/

http://www.pregnancy.com.au/resources/topics-of-interest/labour-and-birth/labour.shtml

http://www.mayoclinic.org/diseases-conditions/postpartum-depression/basics/definition/con-20029130

Made in the USA
San Bernardino, CA
29 February 2020